NETSCAPE ON YOUR LUNCH BREAK

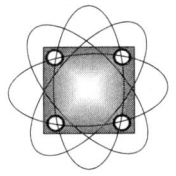

BILL DeRouchey

Discarded

Franklin, Beedle & Associates • 8536 SW St. Helens Dr. • Suite D • Wilsonville, OR 97070

OZARKS REGIONAL LIBRARY
217 EAST DICKSON ST.
FAYETTEVILLE, ARKANSAS 72701

President & Publisher	Jim Leisy (jimleisy@fbeedle.com)
Manuscript Editor	Sheryl Rose
Interior Design & Layout	Karen Foley
Cover Design	Tom Sumner
Proofreader	Susan Skarzynski
Marketing Group	Victor Kaiser
	Sue Page
	Laura Rowe
	Eric Machado
	Cary Crossland
Order Processing	Chris Alarid
	Ann Leisy

Names of all products herein are used for identification purposes only and are trademarks and/or registered trademarks of their respective owners. Franklin, Beedle & Associates, Inc., makes no claim of ownership or corporate association with the products or companies that own them.

© 1997 Franklin, Beedle & Associates Incorporated. No part of this book may be reproduced, stored in a retrieval system, transmitted, or transcribed, in any form or by any means—electronic, mechanical, telepathic, photocopying, recording, or otherwise—without prior written permission of the publisher. Requests for permission should be addressed as follows:

Rights and Permissions
Franklin, Beedle & Associates Incorporated
8536 SW St. Helens Drive, Suite D
Wilsonville, Oregon 97070
http://www.fbeedle.com

CONTENTS

PREFACE	iv
CHAPTER 1—INTRODUCTION	1
CHAPTER 2—NAVIGATING THE WEB	8
CHAPTER 3—CUSTOMIZING THE SCREEN	23
CHAPTER 4—TALKING TECHNICAL	27
CHAPTER 5—BOOKMARKS	32
CHAPTER 6—SEARCHING	35
CHAPTER 7—ADVANCED BOOKMARKS	43
CHAPTER 8—GETTING CLEVER	49
CHAPTER 9—SENDING E-MAIL	56
CHAPTER 10—READING THE NEWS	67
CHAPTER 11—READING E-MAIL	76
CHAPTER 12—FRAMES	79
CHAPTER 13—MULTIMEDIA ON THE WEB	83
APPENDIX A—CONFIGURING MAIL AND NEWS	90
APPENDIX B—PLUG-INS	93
APPENDIX C—NETSCAPE 3.0 MENU OPTIONS	97
GLOSSARY	102
INDEX	105

PREFACE

Let's do lunch! Grab a sandwich and learn about the Internet. All you need is this book, plus some basic computer skills, Internet access, and the ability to log onto it. I'll take it from there.

Netscape on Your Lunch Break is not exhaustive, nor is it meant to be. It is for people who just need a kickstart, who want to learn the basics quickly and then fly on their own. Consider this book your Web training wheels, appropriate as either a self-tutorial or as a part of a software applications course offered by a college.

This book follows the prime directive of fiction: show, don't tell. Rather than just tell about Netscape and the Web and all the neat things you can do, this book shows you how to use Netscape step by step. In the publishing world, we call that "exercise-driven." You'll actually get on the Web, bookmark sites, search on Yahoo!, and send and receive e-mail.

Furthermore, this book will not just teach you how to use Netscape. It will give you background and context into what is happening as you traverse the Web. It even gives you tips on what to do when things go wrong, how to troubleshoot problems using a Web site designed especially for this book. You also learn about advanced Web features such as Java and multimedia.

Even though Navigator is a powerful program, it is easy to learn. Like anything, a bit of practice goes a long way towards proficiency. This book is the perfect tool to get you going. Enjoy!

Acknowledgments

I'd like to thank the Oscar committee. It's an honor just to be nominated. Whoops, wrong speech. It's true what they say: no one person writes a book. Without the help of others, this book wouldn't be here in your hands today.

Thanks to the folks at FBA for all their help. Jim Leisy, for giving me the opportunity to write in the first place. Dawn Groves, Carolyn Gillay, and Pat Sullivan, for showing me what it takes to teach a software application without actually being there. Ernie Ackermann for his experienced insight and solid review of the book. Tom Sumner and Karen Foley, for being the marvelous humans they are. Oh yeah, and for crafting my words into quality and flannel into the cover (finally!).

Thanks to all the folks making the Web a vibrant place to hang out in, virtually. To software companies developing amazing toys. To all the everyday folks building Web sites, whether goofy or stellar, just because they can. To all the system administrators, who never hear when things are going right, only when they're wrong.

Thanks to my family for fostering my curiosity in the first place. To my mom, who taught me to play with words. To my dad, who taught me to tear things apart and put them back together. To my sister Becky, who taught me to stay on my toes.

And lastly, thanks to Samantha, for being my best friend, sounding board, and daily dose of joy.

Bill DeRouchey
Portland, OR

INTRODUCTION

Welcome to the wonderful world of the World Wide Web. Your adventure guides will be Netscape Navigator and this book—the most popular browser for the World Wide Web and the quickest book to teach it to you. In no time you'll be traveling around the world and discovering what is available on the World Wide Web.

The goal of this book is not just to introduce you to the Web, but to teach you the concepts behind it. The book will guide you through the basics of using Netscape Navigator—browsing the Web, searching, and creating bookmarks. You'll send and read e-mail, explore Usenet newsgroups, and learn about new multimedia options such as Java, VRML, and Shockwave. Several appendices offer reference material, including a glossary for the many new terms you'll encounter in the online world. A Web site accompanies this book. Through it you will learn how to improvise when things go wrong. The Web site also provides a collection of links for you to explore.

THE INTERNET

The Internet is a network of networks, a vast collection of computers interconnected globally via various means of telecommunications, millions of files, and an agreed method on how to share them.

CHAPTER 1 INTRODUCTION

Every Internet program, from e-mail to the World Wide Web, began with a few people devising a *protocol* for sharing computer files over existing communications networks. As computing power and modem speeds increased, so did the complexity of computer protocols and accordingly the complexity of the files sent. Now, on the Web, we can download files (pages) with graphics, music, animation, and links to other pages.

Within a few years, we'll probably access the Internet through cable hookups and still complain about slow transfer speeds instead of just marveling at the fact that we can do it at all.

NETSCAPE NAVIGATOR

The World Wide Web was developed by Tim Berners-Lee in 1990 as a means for scientific researchers to share data globally. In the beginning, the Web was text-only and not very flashy. The Web remained so until 1993 when Marc Andreessen, a college student at the University of Illinois, created the first graphical Web browser, NCSA Mosaic. The change was as dramatic as switching from DOS to Windows. The next year, Jim Clark, founder of Silicon Graphics, recruited Andreessen to write Netscape Navigator. As the first graphical browser for the World Wide Web, Mosaic was the initial catalyst for the booming interest in the Web, but Netscape improved on the original and accelerated the boom.

Properly, *Netscape* is the company that publishes *Navigator*, the Web browser, but people tend to refer to *Netscape Navigator* as simply *Netscape*. This distinction was blurry when Navigator was Netscape's only product, but as Netscape continued to develop Internet tools, it began to distinguish the browser from the company. Although both terms are somewhat interchangeable, this book will follow Netscape's convention and refer to the Web browser as *Navigator*.

NETSCAPE ON YOUR LUNCH BREAK

Quick Overview

Note: Your computer should be turned on, but you knew that.

(Windows 95 users) Click the **Start** button, located on the left side of the taskbar. Click **Programs**. Click **Netscape Navigator 3.0**. Click **Netscape Navigator**.

(Windows 3.1 users) If it is not open, double-click the **Netscape** group window. Double-click the **Netscape Navigator** icon.

Navigator opens and displays a page. This default first page is called your *home page*. After you install Navigator, your home page will be the home page of the Netscape Corporation. You will learn how to change this in Chapter 3.

All of the screen images in this book are based on the Windows 95 version of Navigator. Users of Windows 3.1 will be able to follow along without problems because Navigator is virtually identical for both versions of Windows.

Figure 1.1 shows the basic Netscape screen, and important features are noted.

FIGURE 1.1

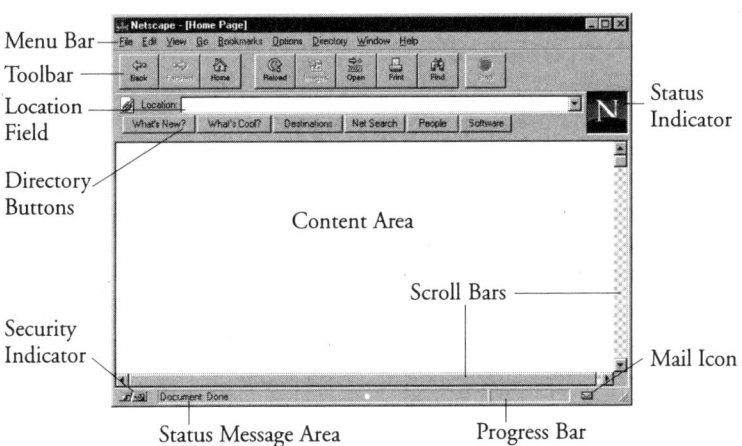

Title Bar

The top line of the Netscape window is the title bar. In this example, it reads *Netscape - [Home Page]*. The title of the current page is displayed in the title bar within the brackets. This page's title is *Home Page*.

Menu Bar

Located directly below the title bar, the menu bar provides nine menus to assist you.

File	Open, close, or exit windows. Save or print files.
Edit	Standard Windows editing options: Undo, Cut, Copy, Paste, and Find.
View	Load images or refresh the current page. View the HTML source code.
Go	Jump back, forward, home, or anywhere along the current path of pages you've visited recently. From here, you can also stop loading the current page.
Bookmarks	Add to or delete from your list of bookmarks. Use them to jump to your favorite sites.
Options	Customize your version of Netscape.
Directory	Use Netscape's online resources.
Window	Open or switch among Netscape Mail, Netscape News, your Bookmarks, Address Book, or History.
Help	Online Help for when you're stuck.

A detailed explanation of each menu item appears in Appendix C.

Toolbar

Below the menu bar are nine buttons to help you navigate through the Web.

Back When possible, jumps back to the previous page.

Forward When possible, jumps forward to the next page.

Home Returns the user to the page loaded upon starting Netscape.

Reload Reaccesses the current page. Used when loading fails.

Images Loads the images for the current page. Only available when Auto Load Images has been turned off.

Open Opens the Open Location dialog box where you can enter a Web address you want to access. Identical to the Location field.

Print Prints the current page.

Find Searches for any word(s) in the current page.

Stop Interrupts the current transfer.

Location Field

The Location field displays the address of the current page that you are viewing. You can access any Web, FTP, or Gopher page by typing its full address (URL) into the Location text box and pressing Enter. Clicking the arrow to the right of the Location field displays the 10 most recently typed addresses.

Directory Buttons

Directory buttons access resources located at Netscape's home page. Each of these resources is also listed under the Directory menu.

Content Area

The content area is where you view the current page.

Status Indicator

The status indicator serves two functions. When Netscape is loading a page, graphic, or anything from the Web, the N animates. The comets zooming past inform you that Netscape is working hard on your request. Clicking the status indicator will load the home page for the Netscape Corporation (http://home.netscape.com). There you will find many resources for finding things on the Web, creating your own pages, or other related information.

Scroll Bars

If a page is wider, or, more likely, taller than the content area, scroll bars appear to help you maneuver up and down or left and right. They function as standard Windows scroll bars. Clicking the up, down, left, and right arrows moves the page slightly in the given direction. Clicking between the arrows and scroll box jumps about a page in the specified direction. Dragging the scroll box moves to an approximate position in the document.

Mail Icons

Clicking the Mail icon opens Netscape Mail. From there you can send or receive e-mail. When you begin a new Netscape session, a question mark appears next to the envelope, telling you that Netscape is not sure if you have new mail or not. If it is configured to do so, Netscape then checks your mail server for new mail. If Netscape finds new mail for you, an exclamation point appears to the right of the envelope. If not, the question mark disappears. Netscape Mail is covered further in Chapter 9.

Progress Bar

As Netscape loads a page, the Progress bar fills from left to right, indicating how far the downloading has progressed.

Status Message Area

The Status Message area serves two main functions. First, it displays the address to which Netscape will jump whenever the cursor is positioned over a link. Second, it provides status information once a link is clicked. You will see Netscape's progress in contacting the appropriate computer, making a connection, and downloading the necessary file(s) in more detail than the Progress bar provides. The Status Message area displays the size of the file that is currently downloading, and often it displays the percentage of its completion.

Security Indicator

Most file transfers over the Web occur without any security protection. In these cases, Netscape displays the security indicator as a broken key against a gray background. This is no reason to panic—the pages you download will rarely contain sensitive information anyway. But in sensitive situations such as online purchases with a credit card, other business transactions, or possibly private communications, Navigator can use higher levels of security. Sites with this capability encrypt your information, such as your credit card number, via complex scrambling methods so that it will only be understood by your copy of Navigator and the server you are connecting to. This prevents your sensitive information from being intercepted online. When this higher level of security is in force, Netscape displays the security indicator as an intact key against a blue background.

Navigating the Web

When Navigator starts, the first page you see is your home page. The term *home page* has two meanings: your initial page upon opening Navigator and the front page of a Web site. When you installed Navigator, your home page was automatically set to the home page of the Netscape Corporation. If you haven't changed it, you see Netscape's home page. You will learn to change this in Chapter 3.

Exploring the Web consists of searching for a subject that interests you, jumping from that page to another, then another, reading, discovering, reacting, watching, jumping to another page, etc. The Web is full of material—some awful, some excellent, and a lot in between. Discovering the good pages is half the fun.

 When you find pages you like, you can create a bookmark to return there easily.

There are four ways to access a page on the Web:

 Click a link. Clicking a link takes you to a new page; this is the most common method. Most pages you access will have links to other pages. Links can be either text or an image. As text, they will be displayed in a different color and often underlined. Images that are links are not as obvious. These require some intuition. If you see several images with descriptive titles or icons, they are probably links.

Type the page's address. Key in the address in the **Location** field and press **Enter**. (You could also click the **Open** button or choose **Open Location** under the **File** menu.) This is useful when you hear of an address in other media. Books, newspaper or magazine articles, and television commercials are listing Web addresses with greater frequency these days. I even saw one on the side of a bus.

Click a bookmark. Netscape provides bookmarks to save addresses of pages you want to return to at a later date. They can be accessed from the Bookmarks menu.

Click a navigation button. The navigation buttons—Back, Forward, and Home—also move you around.

Next we will practice each of these steps. But before that...

A Word of Warning

The World Wide Web is in constant flux. Some sites that we access in this book may have changed slightly since the time of this writing. If a site has changed, you might have to improvise a bit. Chapter 8 will give you some tools for improvising.

Also, the Web and the Internet in general are sometimes unreliable, depending on the time of day, where you are located, or any number of unforeseen factors. What works one minute may not work the next. You may see an error message in the Status Message area stating "Cannot connect to host," a dialog box saying "The server does not have a DNS entry," or nothing at all may happen for minutes. If you receive an error message such as this, calm down, click the Stop button, and try again in a few seconds. If it doesn't work after a few tries, set it aside and come back to it later. This is inherent in working on an international network of networks. Picture the Internet as a freeway system. Some hours are prone to jams. Accidents happen on major roads and side streets. Or the roads could be smooth sailing. There is no way to predict it, so relax and try again later.

CHAPTER 2   NAVIGATING THE WEB

TYPING ADDRESSES AND UNDERSTANDING LINKS

In this exercise, you will visit WebMuseum, an online museum. To do so, you tell Netscape where to find the WebMuseum by entering an address in the Location field. After that, you will learn about links and how to navigate between pages.

1. Click once in the **Netsite** field. It is located directly below the toolbar. The address listed there becomes highlighted.

FIGURE 2.1

> Netsite: http://home.netscape.com/

2. Type **http://www.emf.net/wm/paint/**. Notice that once you begin typing, the label changes to Go to.

FIGURE 2.2

> Go to: http://www.emf.net/wm/paint/

3. Press **Enter** and wait. Notice how the Progress bar fills from left to right and the Status Message area informs you what's happening.

FIGURE 2.3

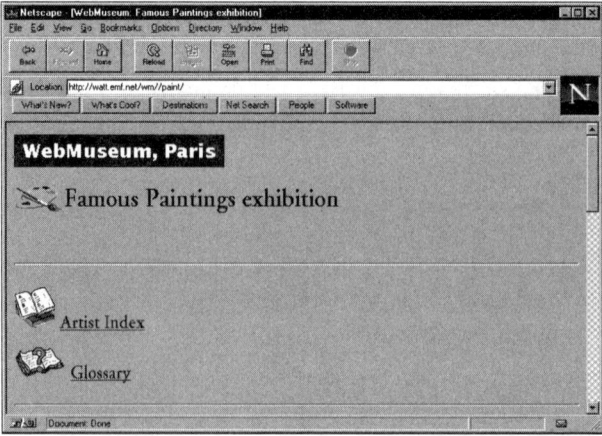

You arrive at the Famous Paintings exhibition of WebMuseum. This is a simple page that includes a few graphics and some text. Two lines, "Artist Index" and "Glossary," are highlighted in blue and underlined (they might be a different color). These *links* allow you to jump to another page by clicking them.

4. Move the mouse pointer over the two links, but do not click yet. The mouse pointer changes from an arrow to a hand. Notice that as you wave over each link, the Status Message area at the bottom of the window changes to reflect the address each link jumps to.

Figure 2.4

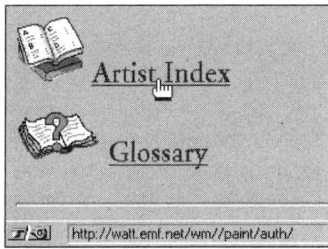 

Each link contains the address for a new page, which is shown in the Status Message area. When you click a link, Netscape reads the address in that link and then searches through the Web for that page. Links can be either text or graphics.

5. Wait until the Status Message reads "Document: Done." Click once in the vertical scroll bar between the scroll box and the bottom arrow. You see the heading "Themes Index." Click the bottom scroll arrow until you see "Fauvism" under the "20th Century" heading. Click **Fauvism**.

CHAPTER 2   NAVIGATING THE WEB

FIGURE 2.5

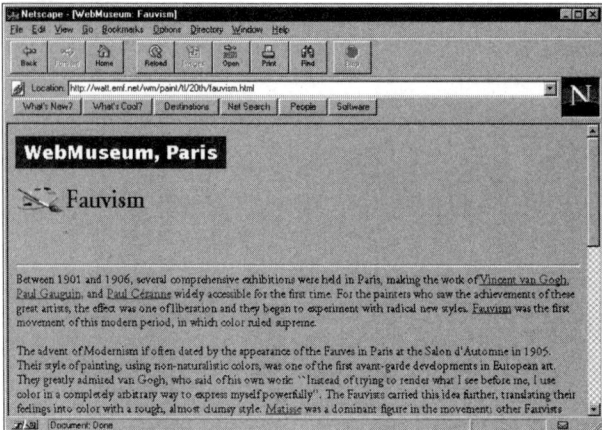

This page details the history of Fauvism.

6 Once the Status Message reads "Document: Done," click **Vincent van Gogh** in the first paragraph.

FIGURE 2.6

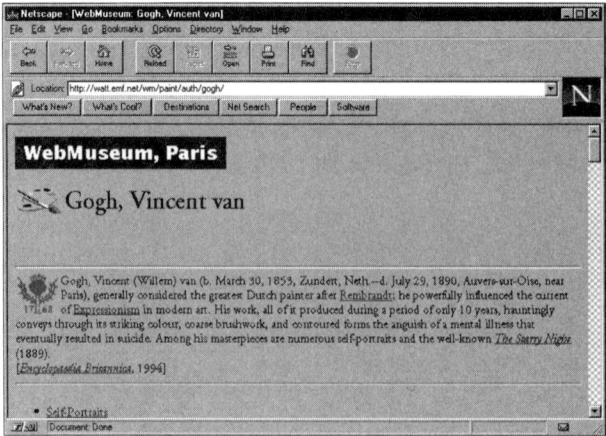

This page details the life of Vincent van Gogh. Vincent was not a happy guy.

7 Once the Status Message reads "Document: Done," click **The Starry Night** in the first paragraph.

FIGURE 2.7

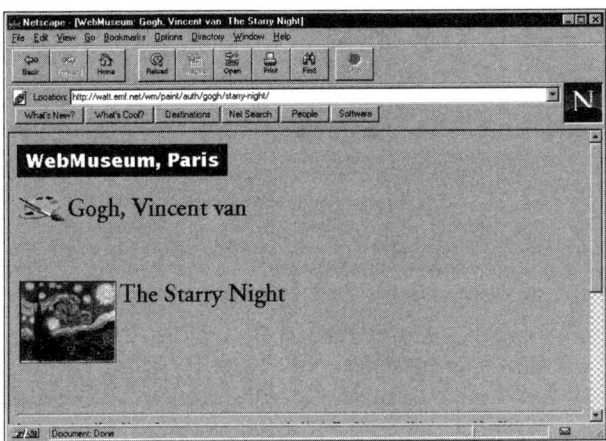

This page details *The Starry Night*, perhaps van Gogh's most famous painting.

USING THE TOOLBAR

Netscape's toolbar provides easy access to the features you will need most often when exploring the Web. In the following steps, you will use the toolbar to continue touring the WebMuseum.

BACK AND FORWARD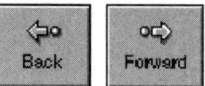

The Back and Forward buttons are guided by Netscape's History. As you jump around the Web, the History records the title and address of each page you visit in order.

8   Click **Window** in the menu bar. Click **History**.

FIGURE 2.8

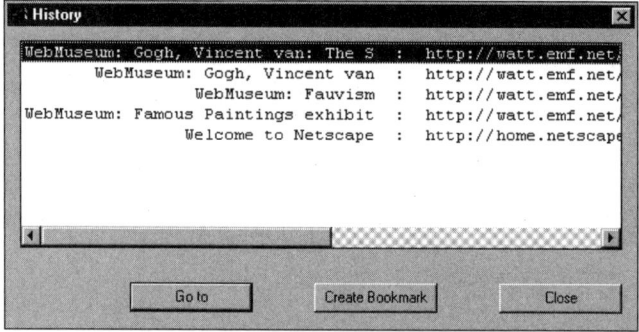

You can see each page that you have visited. Clicking the Back button jumps you one address back (down) in the History, which is the last page you visited. Clicking the Forward button takes you to the next address (up) in the History. Notice that the Forward button is dimmed and unavailable because you are already at the top of the list. The Forward button is unavailable until the Back button has been used.

9   In the History window, click **Close**. In the toolbar, click the **Back** button.

You return to the page on Vincent van Gogh. The Forward button is now available.

10 Click **Window** in the menu bar. Click **History**.

FIGURE 2.9

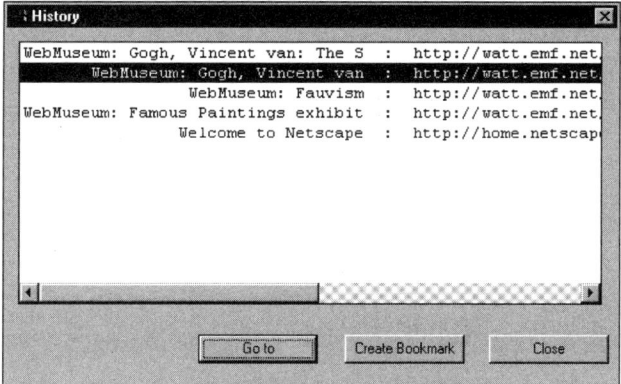

You have moved one address down, or back, in the History.

11 In the History window, click **Close**.

Notice that the *Starry Night* link clicked in step 7 is now a different color. Netscape remembers the addresses of links you've visited and displays them in a different color from links you haven't visited. By default this color is a reddish-purple but it may look different on your system. This color can also be customized (see Chapter 3).

12 Click the **Forward** button.

We return to *The Starry Night*. Notice how the page loaded much faster than before. When Netscape finishes loading a page from the Web, it saves the file describing that page on your hard drive. Now whenever you want to reaccess that page within the current Netscape session, Netscape loads it from the hard drive. The Forward button is unavailable again—we are at the last address in the History.

CHAPTER 2   NAVIGATING THE WEB

 Whereas the History records every page you've visited in the current session, the Go menu lists the pages you've visited recently. This allows you to jump back several pages at once.

13   In the menu bar, click **Go**.

FIGURE 2.10

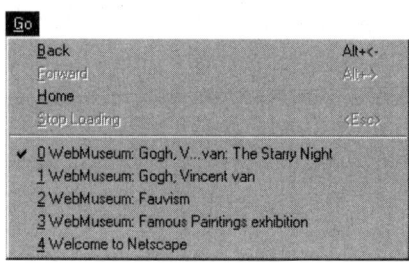

You see the title of each page you've visited in this exercise.

14   Click **3 WebMuseum: Famous Paintings exhibition**.

You've jumped back three pages to the Famous Paintings Exhibition.

15   Scroll up to the top of this page. Click **Artist Index**.

You see the list of available artists.

FIND

The Find button will search for a word(s) in the current page. In long documents such as this Artist Index, Find is invaluable. You will search the Artist Index for Wassily Kandinsky.

16

16 Click the **Find** button.

FIGURE 2.11

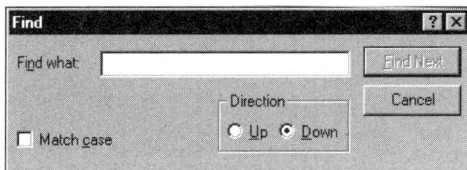

17 In the text box, type **kandinsky**. Click **Find Next**.

FIGURE 2.12

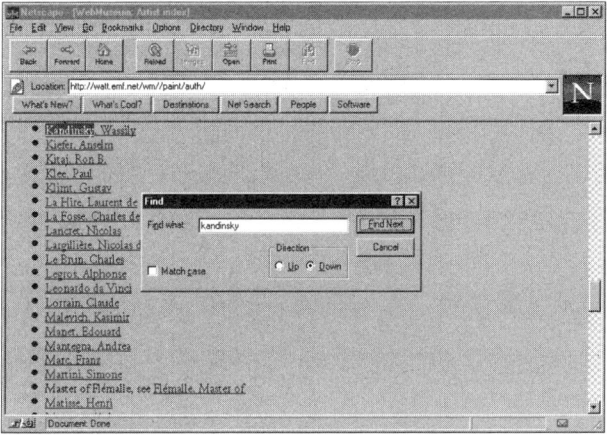

Netscape found the first instance of the word "kandinsky." Notice that the capitalization of "kandinsky" did not matter because the Match Case checkbox was checked off, by default.

18 In the Find window, click **Cancel**.

IMAGES

By default, Netscape automatically downloads all graphics. This can slow down your Web adventuring considerably. You can turn off this feature under the Options menu by clicking Auto Load Images to uncheck it. Once you do, the Images button becomes available to download graphics only when you want to. Images can also be downloaded one at a time.

The Images button is currently unavailable.

19   Click **Options**.

FIGURE 2.13

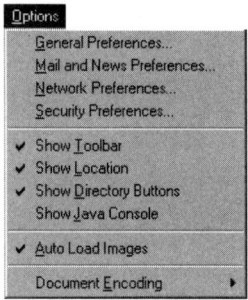

You see the Options menu. From here, you can customize Netscape to your liking. This will be covered further in Chapter 3.

20   Click **Auto Load Images** to turn it off.

The Options menu closes and the Images button is now available. You should still be at the Artist Index listing for Wassily Kandinsky.

21   Click **Kandinsky, Wassily**.

You arrive at the page for Wassily Kandinsky. Even though you switched off automatic downloading of graphics, the first two graphics (WebMuseum Paris and the paintbrush/palette) appear because they were already downloaded on previous pages. When downloading, Netscape first checks to see if the graphic is available on your hard drive in the *cache*. These two were available; others were not.

22 Press the **Page Down** key. Press the **Page Up** key. Press the **Spacebar** twice.

FIGURE 2.14

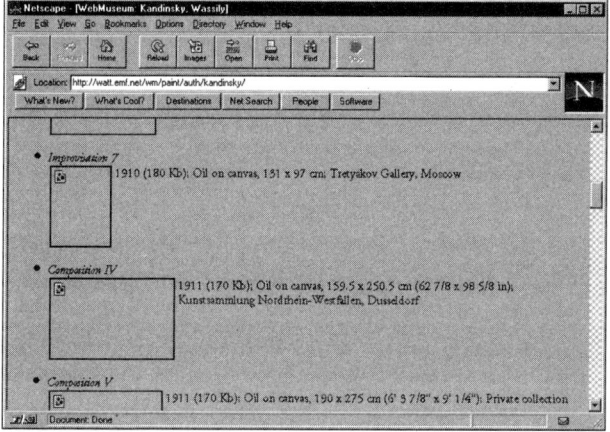

The Page Down and Page Up keys move you up or down one full screen within the current page. The Spacebar also moves you down one full screen. You see three or four outlined empty boxes, each containing a small icon. These icons represent graphics that have not been downloaded. You can download them one at a time or all at once.

23 Under *Improvisation 7*, click the icon inside the box.

FIGURE 2.15

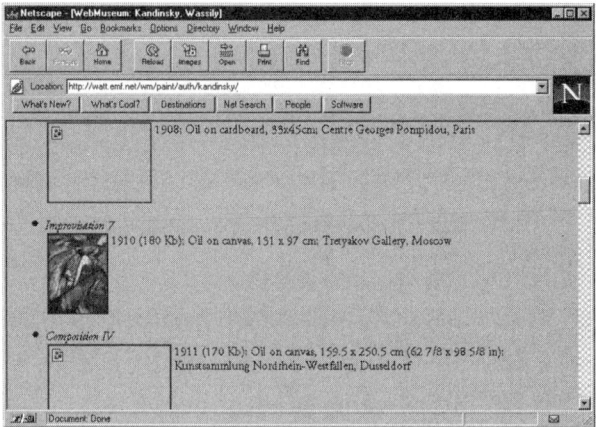

You downloaded only one of the graphics. Clicking the Images button instructs Navigator to load all the images for the current page.

24 In the toolbar, click the **Images** button.

FIGURE 2.16

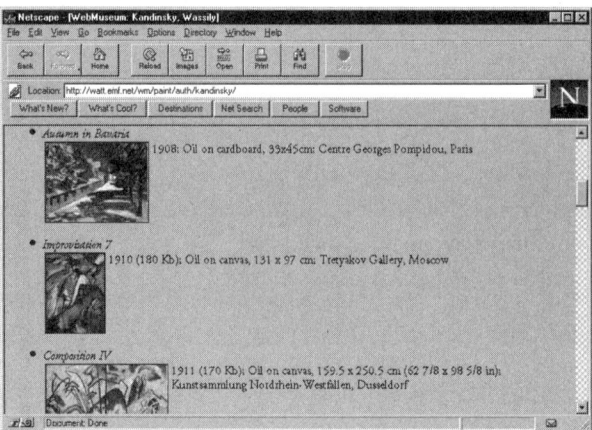

All the graphics on this page are now visible. You can see this by scrolling down the page.

25 Click **Options**. Click **Auto Load Images** to turn it on.

You have restored the autoloading of images.

STOP AND RELOAD

The Stop button simply stops all active downloading.

26 Click the graphic under *Autumn in Bavaria*.

This is a large graphic and will take at least a couple of minutes to download. Suppose you change your mind and don't want to see the entire graphic.

27 Wait until *Autumn in Bavaria* has begun to download. In the toolbar, click the **Stop** button.

Netscape stops downloading and you only see the top portion of *Autumn in Bavaria*.

The Reload button retrieves the current page from the Web again, whether or not it is saved on your hard drive. This may seem pointless, but some Web sites change their content rapidly. But more likely, your current page may get stuck when downloading, due to any random network glitch. In this case, Reload is necessary.

28 Click the **Reload** button.

Netscape begins to reload the current page.

29 Wait until *Autumn in Bavaria* has begun to download. In the toolbar, click the **Stop** button.

OPEN AND PRINT

The only time the Open button is useful is when you have hidden the Location field. Clicking the Open button shows a dialog box in which you can enter an address to be retrieved. However, you can also do this in the Location field below the toolbar. Unless you've hidden the Location field (by clicking off Show Location under the Options menu), you probably won't need the Open button.

The Print button prints the contents of the current page to your default printer. A dialog box appears where you can set the print range or the number of copies to print. Because of the variety of printers, this is left as an exercise for you to explore.

HOME

Clicking the Home button returns you to your home page, the first page opened whenever you start Netscape. This is also the first item in the History. After you install Navigator, your home page will be the home page for the Netscape Corporation (http://home.netscape.com). Changing your home page will be covered in the next chapter.

Customizing the Screen

Netscape provides a lot of flexibility onscreen. You can change colors and fonts, hide toolbars, change your home page. Which features are useful, and which aren't?

Let's tinker with Netscape a bit before we go back online.

Customizing the Toolbars

Depending on your monitor settings, Navigator's toolbars may use a large amount of your screen space.

 Restricting the toolbars will increase the content area for viewing Web pages.

1   Click **Options**.

The top section provides four types of preferences you can change. The second section will show or hide various screen elements. You can show/hide the toolbar, the Location, or the Directory buttons. The Directory buttons are unnecessary since they can be accessed from the Directory menu. You should hide them.

2   Click **Show Directory Buttons** to uncheck it.

If you are using Navigator 2.0, you need to perform one more step.

3 (Navigator 2.0 only) Click **Options**. Click **Save Options**.

The Directory buttons disappear, enlarging the content area.

 Although the toolbar is necessary for your everyday travels, it can be reduced to save more space. By default, the toolbar buttons display both pictures and text. You can change this to display either pictures or text.

4 Click **Options**. Click **General Preferences**. If it is not already selected, click the **Appearance** tab.

FIGURE 3.1

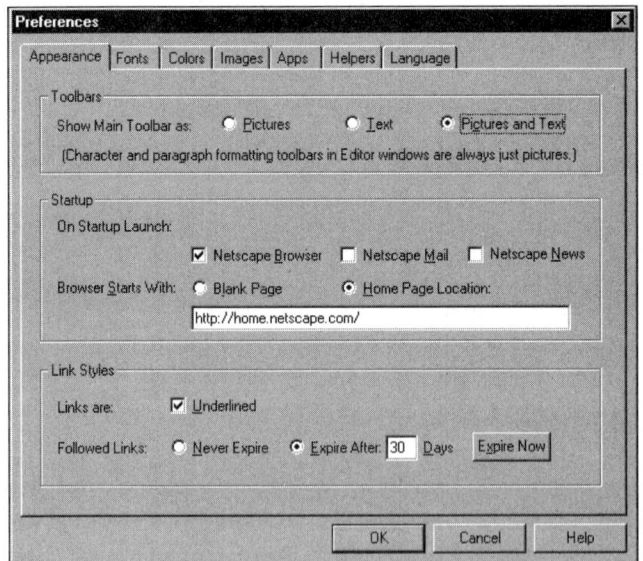

The Preferences dialog box appears. From this dialog box you can customize your copy of Navigator in several ways.

 Choosing **Text** displays the toolbar as:

 Choosing **Pictures** displays the toolbar as:

Although setting the toolbar to text only will save you the most room, you can never see if the Stop button is lit or not. Setting the toolbar to pictures only is my recommendation. Pictures save room, the icons are suitably self-descriptive, and the Stop button lights up.

5 In the Toolbars section, click **Pictures** and click **OK**.

The toolbar changes to pictures only.

Changing Your Home Page

When you begin a Netscape session, the first page loaded into the content area is your *home page*. After installation, your home page will be the home page for the Netscape Corporation. When you want to change this—and you will—choose one that is useful with many links to jump from. In the next exercise, you will change your home page to the online Lunch Break Tutorial.

6 Click **Options**. Click **General Preferences**. If it is not already selected, click the **Appearances** tab.

The Preferences dialog box appears.

CHAPTER 3   CUSTOMIZING THE SCREEN

7   In the text box in the Startup section and under "Browser Starts With," select all the text there and type the following: **http://www.fbeedle.com/lunch/tutorial.html**. Click **OK**.

The Preference dialog box closes, returning you to Navigator.

8   Click the **Home** button.

You arrive at the online Lunch Break Tutorial.

FIGURE 3.2

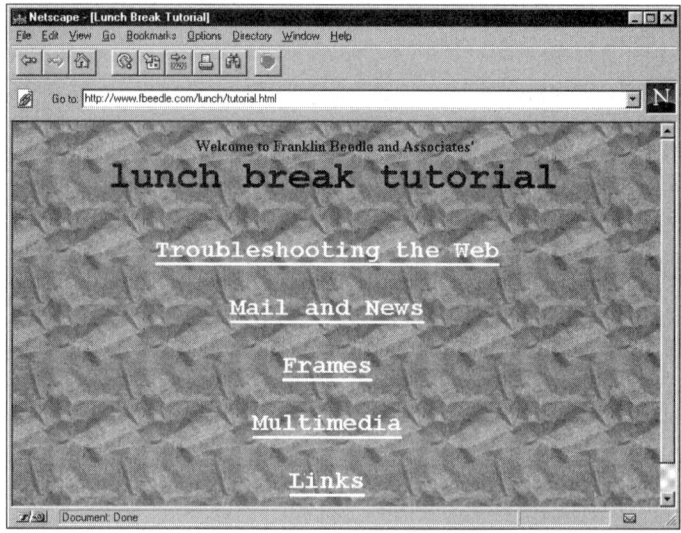

TALKING TECHNICAL

Your future understanding of the Web will be easier if you understand some technical background. How do the Internet and the Web work? What exactly does Navigator do?

UNDERSTANDING ADDRESSES

Every page viewed on the Web is a file stored on a computer somewhere on the Internet. The location of each file is described by its *URL*, or *Uniform Resource Locator*. When you click a link or type an address into Navigator's Location field, Navigator sends a request to the server storing the file. The server then sends the file and Navigator displays it for you.

The URL is structured as: **how://where/what**—*how* the file is to be sent, *where* the file is located, and *what* is the file's name. For example, look back to the address you typed in for the Lunch Break Tutorial: **http://www.fbeedle.com/lunch/tutorial.html**

When you clicked this link, Navigator read the URL embedded in that link and dissected it into three sections.

The first section, everything before the **://**, tells Navigator how the file should be retrieved. In this case it is *http, hypertext transfer protocol*, a description of how files are sent and received via the World Wide Web. Other likely protocols here are *ftp (file transfer protocol)* and *gopher*.

The second section, between the **://** and the first forward slash **/**, tells Navigator which computer the file is stored on, in this case, **www.fbeedle.com**. The domain name identifies a particular computer on the Internet. This is explained further in the next section.

The last section represents where the file is located on the server. Subsequent forward slashes list subdirectories that lead to the file; there is only one in this case: **lunch**. Lastly, the name of the file follows the final forward slash: **tutorial.html**.

Once Navigator reads these three sections, it sends into the Internet a request to "www.fbeedle.com" to send via "http" the "tutorial.html" file located in the "lunch" directory.

Confused? Let's try an analogy. Suppose you wanted to order those fuzzy slippers from page 39 of the Galactic Footware catalog. To order them, you need to drop a postcard into a mailbox. The card should include your return address and the following order:

fedex://galactic.footware/page39/fuzzy.slippers

This instructs galactic.footware (where) to send via fedex, or Federal Express, (how) the fuzzy.slippers (what) found on page39. Galactic Footware automatically knows to send the fuzzy slippers to your address because it was included with your request.

Domain Names

Each computer on the Internet is assigned an *Internet Protocol address*, or *IP address*, a numerical sequence such as 238.162.97.134. Since users are unlikely to remember these sequences, each computer is also assigned a *domain name* that corresponds to an IP address. Domain names are character-based, such as www.hampton.com, and thus easier for us to remember. The cross-referencing of IP address to domain name will be invisible to you.

You will often see the tilde character (~) in web addresses, such as http://www.hampton.com/~charlie. The tilde represents someone who has an account on a network. In this case "charlie" has an account on "hampton.com." Thus, if you know someone's e-mail address, you can guess their web address fairly easily. Suppose your friend's e-mail address is barnaby@jones.com. To build their web address, start with "http://" since you know that all web addresses begin with this. You can guess that the server is "www.jones.com" since most domain names begin with "www." Add a slash, a tilde, and "barnaby" and you get "http://www.jones.com/~barnaby." This method will almost always work. If it doesn't, you can just e-mail your friend and ask!

You've probably noticed that most domain names end in ".com." This suffix represents a commercial enterprise. Following is a table of other suffixes you might see and examples of them:

com	commercial enterprise	www.bowling.com
edu	educational institution	cs.mit.edu
gov	governmental department	nasa.gov
mil	military	army.mil
net	network	tennis.net
org	noncommercial organization	monkey.localzoo.org

Two-letter combinations represent countries. Country codes you might see on the Web are:

aq	Antarctica	ie	Ireland
at	Austria	in	India
au	Australia	il	Israel
be	Belgium	it	Italy
br	Brazil	jp	Japan
ca	Canada	mx	Mexico
cn	China	nl	Netherlands
ch	Switzerland	no	Norway
cz	Czech Republic	np	Nepal
de	Germany	ru	Russian Federation
dk	Denmark	se	Sweden
eg	Egypt	tr	Turkey
es	Spain	tw	Taiwan
fi	Finland	uk	United Kingdom
fr	France	us	United States

HTML

Each page you see on the Web is written in *HTML, Hypertext Markup Language*. Web browsers such as Navigator interpret these plain text files into what you see on the screen. This section will introduce you to the basics of HTML.

1. If the Lunch Break Tutorial page is not displayed, click the **Home** button. Click **View**. Click **Document Source**.

FIGURE 4.1

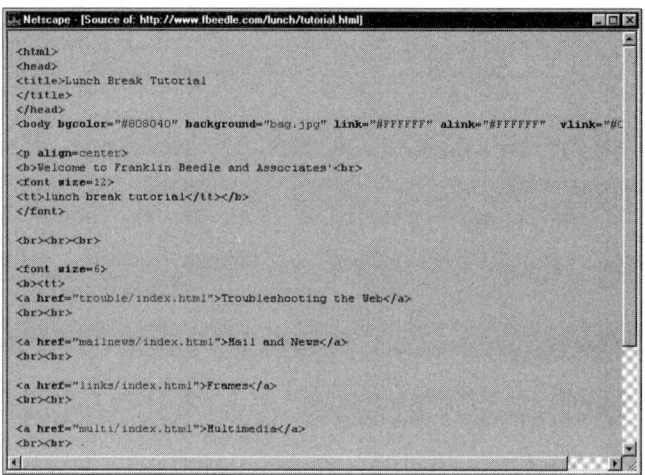

Navigator opens a new window and displays the text file that represents the Lunch Break Tutorial. You see a lot of pairs of codes in brackets such as <b> and </b>, <body> and </body>, or <a href> and </a>. If you are familiar with word processing, especially WordPerfect 5.1, you should recognize the concept of using tags to describe text. Tags in HTML tell Navigator, or any web browser, how to display the text within each pair of tags. For example, any text between <b> and </b> will be **boldfaced**. Any text between <a href> and </a> will be a link. (The "a" stands for anchor and the "href" stands for hypertext reference.)

2. Look at the line that reads "<a href="trouble/index.html">Troubleshooting the Web</a>."

This is the description of a link. The surrounding <a href> and </a> tags tell Navigator to make the words "Troubleshooting the Web" a link to the file "trouble/index.html".

3. Press **Alt** + **Tab** to return to the Navigator window. Hold the mouse pointer over the "Troubleshooting the Web" link.

The status bar reads "http://www.fbeedle.com/lunch/trouble/index.html".

You should now roughly understand the basics of HTML. At this point, that's all you need. Even this little bit of knowledge will help you in Chapter 8 where you learn how to solve problems when things go wrong.

5

BOOKMARKS

Even though you do need to understand how Web addresses work, you don't want to type them every time you want to access a page. If you wanted to visit the *New York Times* site daily, would you want to type its address every day?

Netscape provides bookmarks for you to mark pages you want to return to. Once created, bookmarks are just two clicks away in the Bookmarks menu. If your list of bookmarks becomes long and unmanageable, you can categorize them for easy reference.

tip Adding bookmarks is absolutely necessary for using the Web efficiently.

In this exercise, you will visit three search engines, Yahoo!, Lycos, and AltaVista, and record a bookmark for each.

Note: This exercise assumes you have no existing bookmarks. If you do, the figures in this chapter will not exactly match yours.

CREATING BOOKMARKS

1 In the **Location** field, type **http://www.yahoo.com** and press **Enter**.

You arrive at Yahoo!

2. Wait until Yahoo! is displayed. Click **Bookmarks** in the menu bar.

FIGURE 5.1

3. Click **Add Bookmark**.

You have added a bookmark for Yahoo!

4. Click **Bookmarks**.

FIGURE 5.2

Yahoo! appears at the bottom of the bookmark list.

5. Click **Bookmarks**.

The Bookmarks menu is deselected. There is a faster way to create a bookmark. Let's visit our second search engine, Lycos.

6. In the **Location** text box, type **http://www.lycos.com** and press **Enter**. Wait until Lycos is displayed. Press **Ctrl + D**.

You created a bookmark for Lycos.

7. Click **Bookmarks**.

FIGURE 5.3

CHAPTER 5   BOOKMARKS

Welcome to Lycos appears at the bottom of the bookmark list.

8   Click **Bookmarks**.

The Bookmarks menu is deselected. There is a third way to create a bookmark. Let's visit our last search engine, AltaVista.

9   In the **Location** text box, type **http://www.altavista.digital.com** and press **Enter**. Wait for AltaVista to begin displaying. Click the *right* mouse button.

FIGURE 5.4

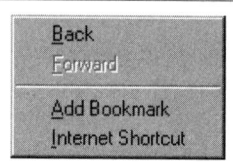

```
Back
Forward
Add Bookmark
Internet Shortcut
```

A pop-up menu appears.

10   Click **Add Bookmark**.

You have created a bookmark for AltaVista. It's that easy! You have learned three methods to create bookmarks for the most popular searching sites. Let's learn how to use them.

SEARCHING

To research a particular subject among the millions of pages on the Web, you will need to use a *search engine*. A search engine is a site that has compiled massive listings of pages on the World Wide Web. Using a search engine makes it easier to sift through all that information for the subjects you want.

All search engines operate similarly. You enter the keyword(s) you wish to search for and click a button labeled Search, Find, Submit, or something similar. The search engine returns to you each successful match, or *hit*, to your keyword. However, results are returned in two different ways. The first method is by category—hits are grouped alphabetically by category or title. The second is by score—hits are ranked by the frequency of the keyword(s) within the match. Yahoo! is the best example of reporting results by category. Lycos and AltaVista report results by score. Since no single search engine indexes the entire World Wide Web, the best strategy is to use as many as possible. We will explore all three.

1   Click **Bookmarks**. Click **Yahoo!**

FIGURE 6.1

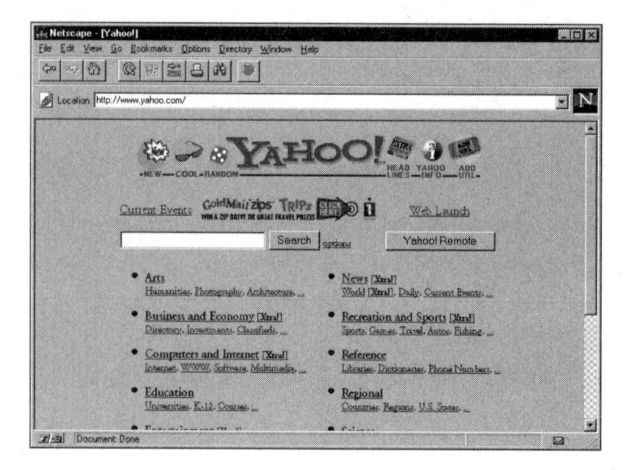

Netscape retrieves the file located at the address saved under the Yahoo! bookmark. It is the Yahoo! home page. At the top of Yahoo!'s page are six buttons to aid you. From left to right: New displays a categorized list of all new sites, Cool displays sites determined cool by Yahoo!, Random takes you to a random site, Headlines displays current news of the world, Yahoo Info displays general information on Yahoo!, and Add URL provides a method to add a new site to Yahoo!'s listings.

Below are many categories of sites. You can peruse these or search for a specific site by using the simple form located in the middle of the page. *Forms* allow you to interact with the server on the other end. You enter information into text boxes, check boxes, and radio buttons. Click a button to send the information to the server. The server processes your input and replies with a response appropriate to the form.

NETSCAPE ON YOUR LUNCH BREAK

Let's start searching. Suppose you are a big fan of ping-pong. Do you think anything on ping-pong exists on the Web?

2   In the text box, type **ping-pong** and click **Search**.

FIGURE 6.2

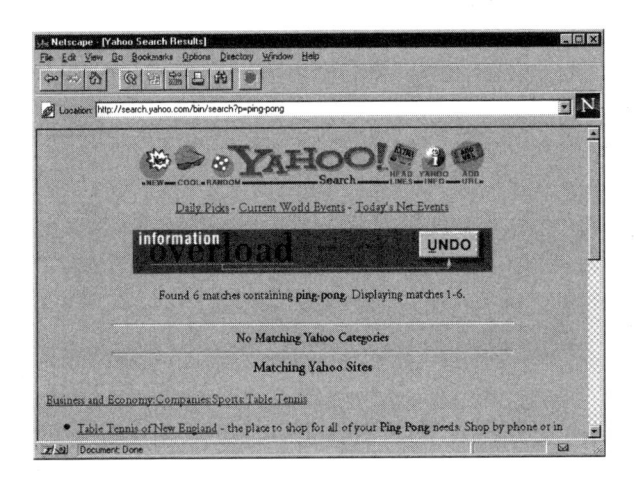

Yahoo! hunts through its database and returns several entries containing "ping" and "pong" (six at the time of this writing). Notice that Yahoo! ignored the dash between the two words. Looking at the list, you realize that you can also search on "table tennis."

3   Scroll to the bottom of the page. There should be a text box containing the text of your original search. With the mouse, select **ping-pong** so that it is highlighted, and type **table tennis**. Click **Search**.

FIGURE 6.3

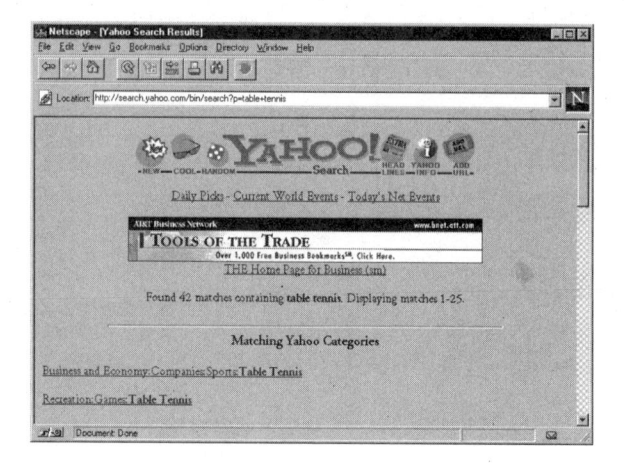

Much better. You have 42 entries containing "table tennis," including two entire categories. Searching successfully on the Web requires you to be clever and versatile. In the above example, you used another term for "ping-pong" to find more results. That was clever; now let's be versatile and search elsewhere.

4 Click **Bookmarks**. Click **Welcome to Lycos**.

FIGURE 6.4

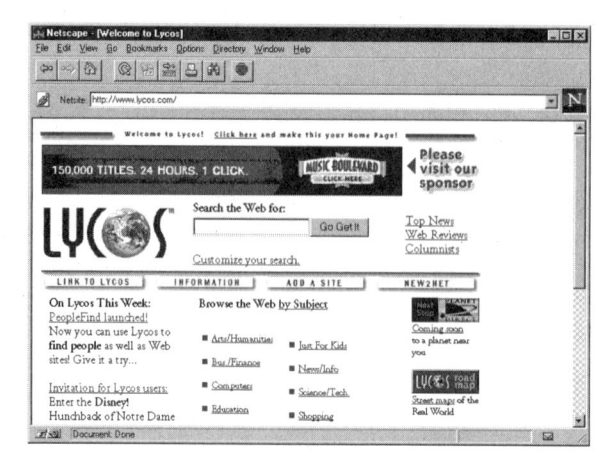

A text box for entering your keyword(s) is surrounded by a lot of options.

5 In the text box, type **ping-pong** and click the **Go Get It** button.

FIGURE 6.5

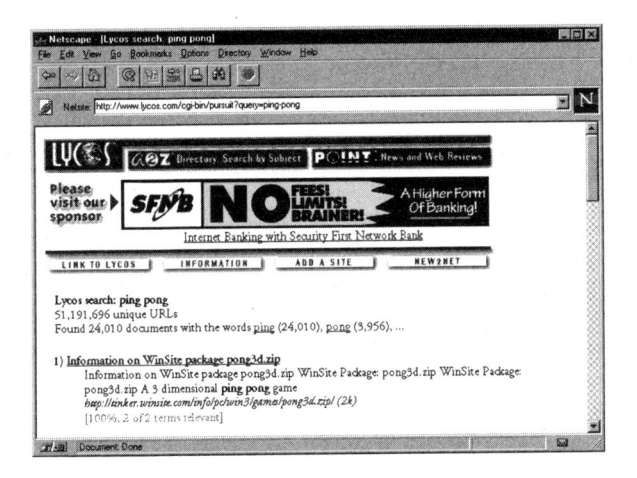

Lycos returns an entirely different set of results. At first glance, it seems that this page lists many more hits than Yahoo! did. This doesn't necessarily mean that Lycos is better, but it does suggest that you should use as many search engines as possible.

Because Lycos ranks results by how many times your keyword(s) appear on a page, the hits will display completely differently from Yahoo!'s alphabetical order. Lycos's results are also usually larger, because of how Yahoo! and Lycos gather information. Yahoo! fills its listings through submissions only. The author of a Web site submits to Yahoo! the address of the site and the appropriate category. Lycos builds its listings through programs called robots, infobots, or spiders. These programs travel around the Web, collect information on any pages found, and send the results back to Lycos. AltaVista works similarly.

CHAPTER 6   SEARCHING

6   Click **Bookmarks**. Click **AltaVista**.

FIGURE 6.6

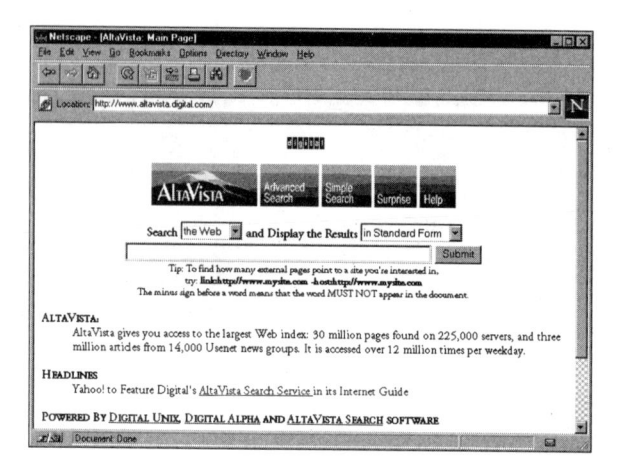

You arrive at AltaVista, another premiere search engine. From here, you will attempt a more advanced search.

7   In the toolbar at the top, click **Advanced Search**.

FIGURE 6.7

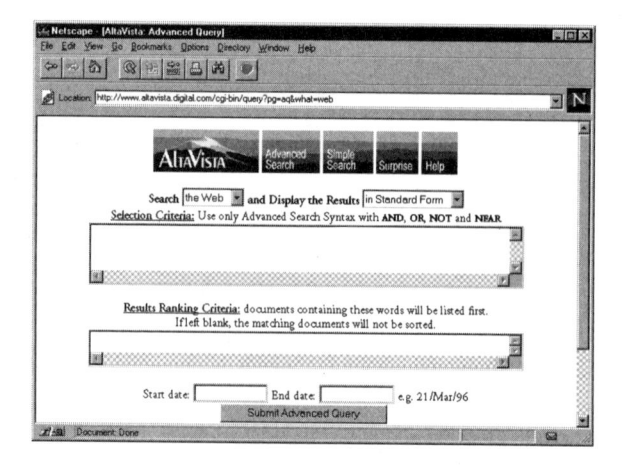

NETSCAPE ON YOUR LUNCH BREAK

This page provides flexibility in your search. You can use simple logic statements to include this AND that OR that.

8   In the text box below "Results Ranking Criteria," type the following, including the quotation marks: **"table tennis" OR "ping-pong"**

9   Click **Submit Advanced Query**.

FIGURE 6.8

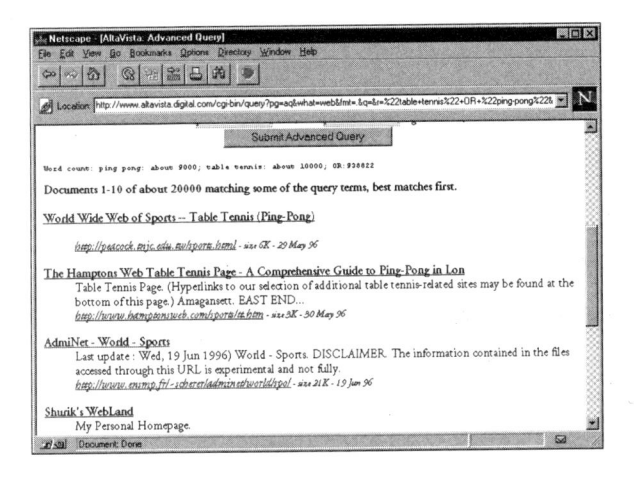

AltaVista returns a list similar to the one Lycos returned, except AltaVista was able to search for results for both "table tennis" and "ping pong." Let's visit a site. In this example, the first site listed is the "World Wide Web of Sports — Table Tennis (Ping-Pong)." Yours may be different.

10   Click the first site listed in your list.

41

FIGURE 6.9

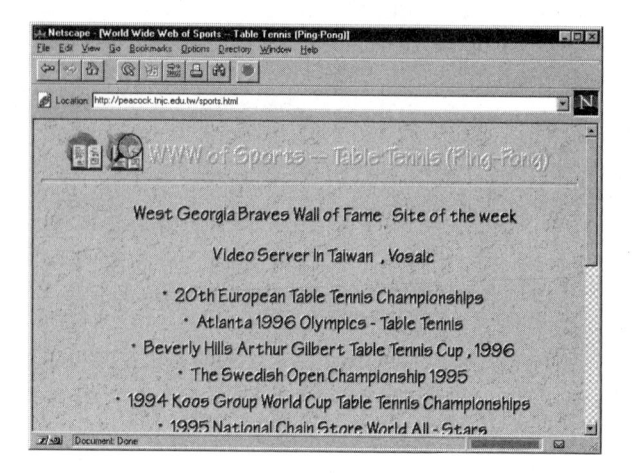

You've visited the ping-pong site listed first from your AltaVista search.

11   Press **Ctrl + D**. Click **Bookmarks**.

You have added a bookmark and can see it in your bookmark list. In the next chapter, you will learn how to delete this bookmark.

12   Click **Bookmarks**.

The Bookmarks menu is deselected.

A Note on Copyrights

It is tempting to use material found on the Web. However, most information on the Web is copyrighted, meaning that you cannot use it verbatim. Treat material on the Web as if you found it in an encyclopedia—read it, digest it, and apply any pertinent information to your research at hand. For photos or other images, write down the copyright notice and place it next to the image in your research paper.

Advanced Bookmarks

Now that you can conduct a search and create bookmarks, you need to learn how to organize your list of bookmarks.

Organizing Bookmarks

Adding bookmarks is absolutely necessary for using the Web efficiently, but even more important is organizing the bookmarks you have.

> **tip:** Without organization, your bookmark list will be long and random. Organized, your Web adventures will be a breeze.

You will create a folder for the three search engine bookmarks you have already created.

1 Click **Bookmarks**. Click **Go to Bookmarks**.

Figure 7.1

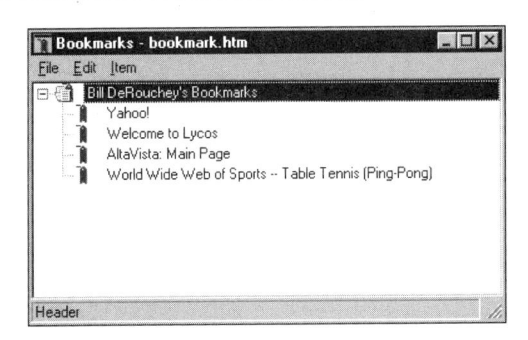

CHAPTER 7   ADVANCED BOOKMARKS

Your list of bookmarks appears.

2   Click **Item**. Click **Insert Folder**.

FIGURE 7.2

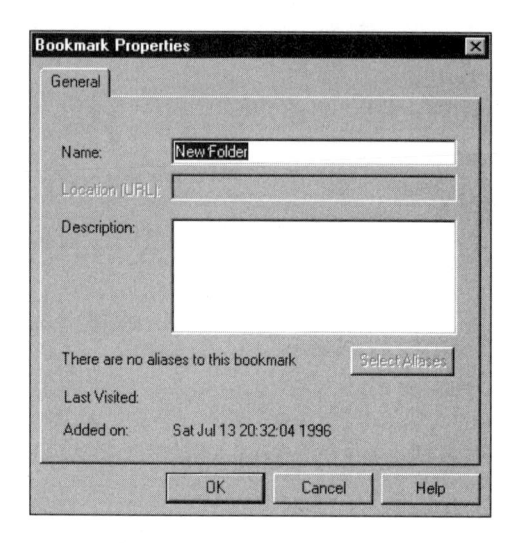

The Bookmark Properties dialog box opens.

3   In the **Name** text box, which should already be highlighted, type **Searchers**. Click **OK**.

FIGURE 7.3

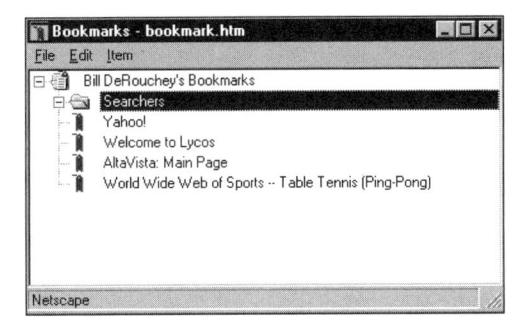

```
Bookmarks - bookmark.htm
File  Edit  Item
  Bill DeRouchey's Bookmarks
    Searchers
      Yahoo!
      Welcome to Lycos
      AltaVista: Main Page
      World Wide Web of Sports -- Table Tennis (Ping-Pong)

Netscape
```

The Searchers folder appears at the top of the list. You can now put your new bookmarks in the Searchers folder.

4 Move the mouse pointer to the **Yahoo!** bookmark. Press down and *do not release* the left mouse button. The Yahoo! bookmark should be highlighted. While continuing to hold down the left mouse button, move the mouse pointer to the **Searchers** folder until it is highlighted. Release the mouse button.

FIGURE 7.4

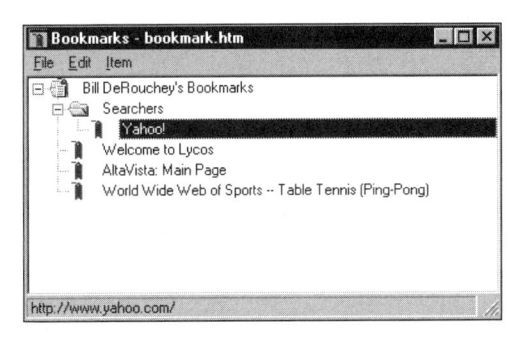

```
Bookmarks - bookmark.htm
File  Edit  Item
  Bill DeRouchey's Bookmarks
    Searchers
      Yahoo!
      Welcome to Lycos
      AltaVista: Main Page
      World Wide Web of Sports -- Table Tennis (Ping-Pong)

http://www.yahoo.com/
```

You dragged the Yahoo! bookmark into the Searchers folder. It now appears in the list under the Searchers folder.

5. Drag the **Lycos** and **AltaVista** bookmarks into the **Searchers** folder.

FIGURE 7.5

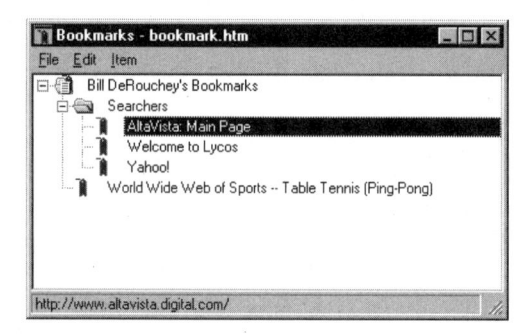

You have created bookmarks for three search engines and saved them in a single folder. The "Welcome to" in the "Welcome to Lycos" bookmark seems excessive. You will edit it.

6. Move the mouse pointer to the **Lycos** bookmark and click the *right* mouse button once.

FIGURE 7.6

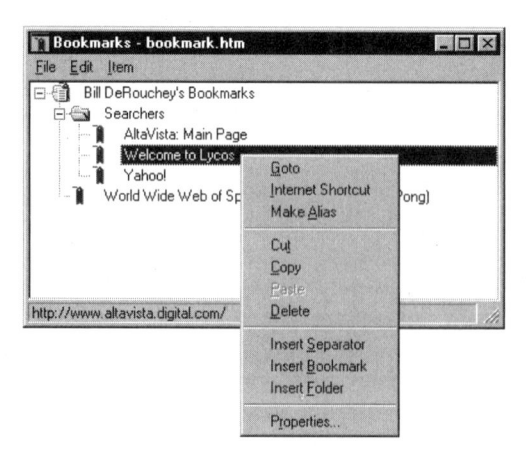

A pop-up menu appears. From here, you could either jump to this bookmark or edit its properties.

7   Click **Properties**.

FIGURE 7.7

The Bookmark Properties dialog box opens. You see the title and Web address for Lycos.

8   In the **Name** text box (which should be already highlighted), type **Lycos**. Click **OK**.

FIGURE 7.8

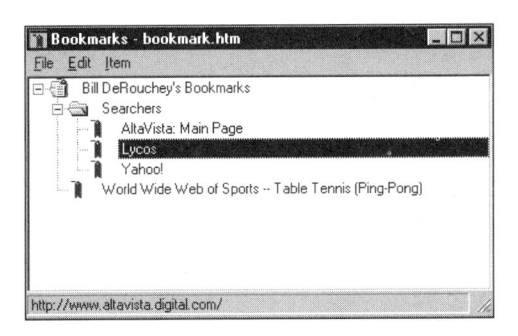

You changed the title for this bookmark and can see it under the Searchers folder. It is now tidy.

CHAPTER 7   ADVANCED BOOKMARKS

You can also delete bookmarks if you no longer need them.

9   Click on the **ping-pong** bookmark you created at the end of the last chapter. In this example, it is **World Wide Web of Sports — Table Tennis (Ping-Pong)**. Press the **Delete** key.

FIGURE 7.9

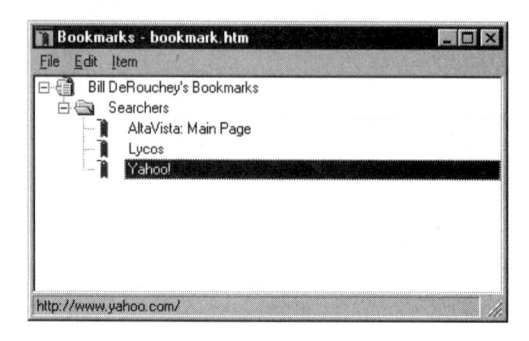

You deleted the ping-pong bookmark.

10   In the Netscape Bookmarks window, click **File**. Click **Close**.

The Bookmarks window closes and you return to the main Netscape window.

11   Click **Bookmarks**. Click **Searchers**.

FIGURE 7.10

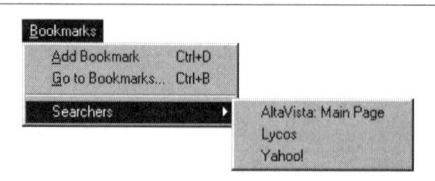

You see your searching bookmarks organized into a single folder. Notice also that the ping-pong bookmark is gone.

12   Click **Bookmarks**.

The Bookmarks menu is deselected.

Getting Clever

Once you learn how to use Navigator well, or any piece of software, you learn to improvise, to be clever. When jumping around the Web, you will undoubtedly encounter problems. Links lead to missing pages. Huge images slow you down. Servers don't respond. Is there anything you can do? We will examine several problem situations and discover when cleverness can circumvent them.

"Netscape is unable to locate the server..."

FIGURE 8.1

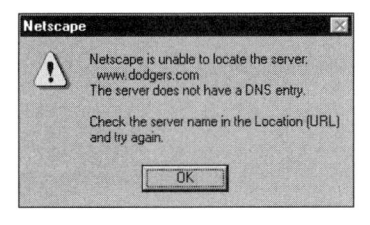

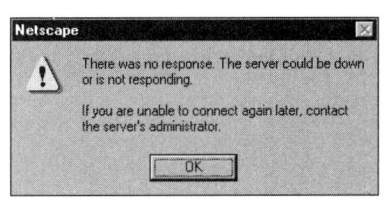

Servers sometimes lose their connection to the Internet, despite the best of intentions. Anything can cause a computer to shut down—power outages, system overload, scheduled maintenance, floods. The NASDAQ stock market was shut down for a day last year when squirrels ate through some power cables. In these cases, all you can do is try again later.

One exception is when the name of the server is misspelled in the link. In this example, if the true name of the server was "www.dodjers.com" but the link read "www.dodgers.com," Navigator would not be able to locate the misspelled server name. You will learn how to fix this later in this chapter.

"File Not Found" or "404 Not Found"

This is the error message you will probably see most often. This usually means that no page exists at the requested address. Either the page has been moved or deleted since a link to it was created, or the link itself has an error. If the problem is a mistyped link, you can work around the problem with a little luck and intuition.

1   In Navigator's toolbar, click the **Home** button.

You arrive at the Lunch Break Tutorial site.

2   Click **Troubleshooting the Web**.

A list of problems appears.

3   Click **Problem #1**.

Figure 8.2

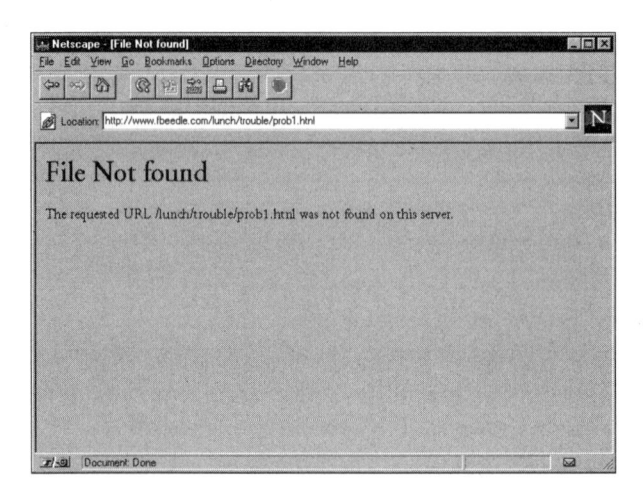

Navigator locates the server and sends your request. The server replies that the file does not exist. The address that you attempted to load is listed in the Location text box. In these situations, you should inspect the address to see if you can fix it before moving on. Read the address. Are there any obvious problems? This address ends with ".htnl" even though every address we have seen so far ends with ".html". You can easily fix this.

4   Click once in the **Location** field.

The entire address is selected.

5   Click once after the end of the address.

The address is deselected and the cursor is at the end.

6   Press the left arrow key once to move back one character. Press the **Backspace** key once to delete the letter **n**. Press the **m** key. The address should read "...html". Press **Enter**.

Bingo. Navigator retrieves the page that the link was *supposed* to represent, except for the mistyped address.

7   Click **Return to Troubleshooting**.

You return to the Troubleshooting Tutorial page. Let's try something more difficult.

8   Click **Problem #2**.

FIGURE 8.3

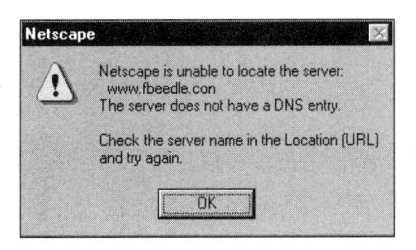

CHAPTER 8   GETTING CLEVER

Navigator tells you it can't locate the server. Normally, this would mean that the server you are trying to access is down for some reason. But this could also be a mistyped link.

> **tip:** You can inspect the link in the status bar by moving the mouse pointer over the link.

9   Click **OK** to close the warning box. Hold the mouse pointer over the **Problem #2** link. Look at the status bar.

Whoops. The domain name is "www.fbeedle.con." Since nearly every domain name ends with ".com" this must be a mistake. The link itself cannot be fixed. However, we can cleverly work around it.

10 With the mouse pointer still positioned on the **Problem #2** link, click the *right* mouse button.

FIGURE 8.4

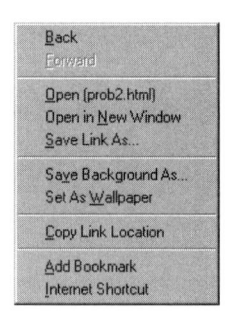

```
Back
Forward

Open (prob2.html)
Open in New Window
Save Link As...

Save Background As...
Set As Wallpaper

Copy Link Location

Add Bookmark
Internet Shortcut
```

A pop-up menu appears.

11 Click **Copy Link Location**.

The address contained in the link has been copied to the Clipboard. You can now simply paste it anywhere.

12 Click in the **Location** text box to highlight all the text there. Click **Edit**. Click **Paste**.

The address from the bad link now appears in the Location field. Let's stop for a second and notice what you've done. When you click a link, Navigator copies the address in the link to a section of its memory, prepares it for sending, and sends the request to the address. You have done the same thing, step by step. You copied the address to the Clipboard and pasted it in the Location field. The address is ready to go. However, this method allows you the luxury of editing the address before you send it.

The cursor is at the end of the address within the Location field.

13 Click the cursor after **.con**. Press the **Backspace** key to delete the **n**. Press the **m** key. The address should read "...www.fbeedle.com...". Press **Enter**.

Navigator retrieves the page that the link was *supposed* to represent, except for the mistyped domain name.

These methods of editing links will not work every time, but they're a good place to start.

Emptying the Cache

When you access pages on the Web, Navigator downloads each file and image and stores them on your computer as temporary files in a directory called the *cache*. If a requested file or image exists in the cache from a previous download, then Navigator can retrieve it from the cache without needing to download it from the Web. This saves time if you access certain pages often.

However, these files consume disk space. By default, Navigator reserves only 5000 kilobytes for the cache. When this limit is approached, Navigator can no longer cache pages, slowing down your Web excursions.

> **tip** To avoid running out of disk space, you should empty the cache occasionally.

14 Click **Options**. Click **Network Preferences**. If it is not already selected, click the **Cache** tab.

CHAPTER 8   GETTING CLEVER

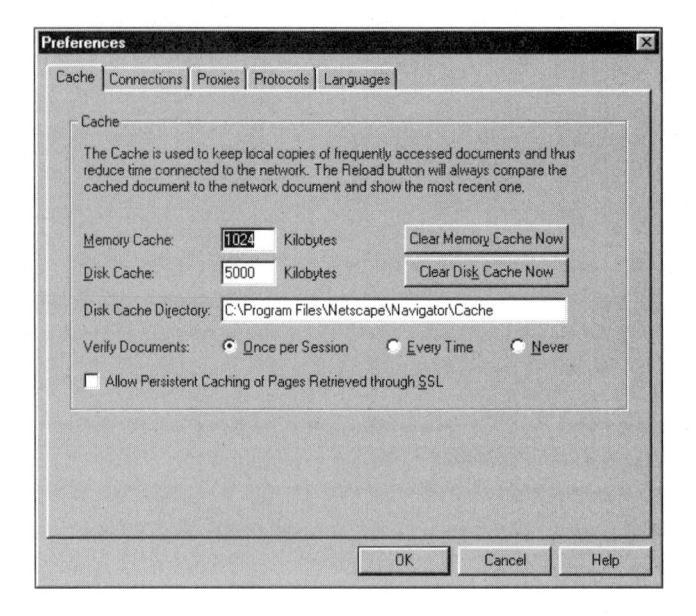

FIGURE 8.5

[Preferences dialog box showing Cache tab with Memory Cache: 1024 Kilobytes, Disk Cache: 5000 Kilobytes, Disk Cache Directory: C:\Program Files\Netscape\Navigator\Cache, Verify Documents: Once per Session, with Clear Memory Cache Now and Clear Disk Cache Now buttons]

The network Preferences dialog box opens. From here you can clear the disk cache or change the cache size or location.

15   Click **Clear Disk Cache Now**.

FIGURE 8.6

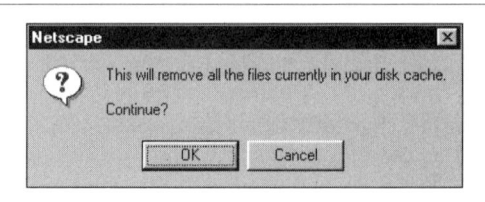

[Netscape dialog: "This will remove all the files currently in your disk cache. Continue?" with OK and Cancel buttons]

Navigator double-checks your request.

54

16 Click **OK**.

Navigator deletes all the files you previously downloaded, such as the Kandinsky images in Chapter 2, the pages at Yahoo!, or anything else you might have accessed recently.

17 Click **OK** to close the Preferences dialog box.

You return to the Troubleshooting Tutorial.

Shortcuts

Navigator accepts a couple of shortcuts when entering URLs.

18 In the **Location** text box, type **www.cnn.com** and press **Enter**.

You arrive at the CNN home page. If you do not include the "how://" portion of the URL as described in Chapter 4, Navigator assumes it should begin with "http://".

19 In the **Location** text box, type **usatoday** and press **Enter**.

Watch the status bar. When Navigator is unable to find "usatoday," it assumes you are looking for "www.usatoday.com". You successfully arrive at USA Today.

This shortcut can be extended. "http://www.hampton.com/~charlie" can be entered as "hampton/~charlie". "http://www.microsoft.com/excel" could be entered as "microsoft/excel". Navigating the Web keeps getting easier.

9

SENDING E-MAIL

With Netscape Navigator, you can do more than just browse the Web. You can also read articles in Usenet newsgroups and exchange e-mail. We will discuss Usenet newsgroups in the next chapter. First, however, you must configure Netscape to retrieve mail and news properly. Please consult Appendix A, "Configuring Mail and News," before proceeding.

"E-mail" is short for electronic mail, an electronic version of the traditional postal system where messages (letters) arrive in seconds instead of days. Messages are sent from and received at the address that every user must have in order to access the Internet. If you've been able to perform the previous exercises, you must have an e-mail address, such as *you@bigcomputer.com*.

In this exercise, you will send e-mail. You can access Netscape Mail in two ways. The first is to click Window and click Netscape Mail. You will do the second, which is easier.

1   Click the **Mail** icon located at the bottom right of the Netscape window.

The Netscape Mail window opens. Depending on your configuration, you probably saw other dialog boxes before this window opened. If Netscape told you that configuration information was missing, you need to consult Appendix A, "Configuring Mail and News," before continuing. This lets Netscape know where to find your mail.

Netscape also may have asked you for your password. If so, enter the password and click OK. Passwords are nearly always case-sensitive, so be sure your CapsLock key is not on. TOPSECRET and TopSecret are not the same password.

If everything was configured properly, Netscape logged on, and it either downloaded all new messages or it informed you that you have no new messages on the server. There is probably a welcome message from Mozilla, Netscape's mascot. Figure 9.1 shows the main features of the Mail window.

FIGURE 9.1

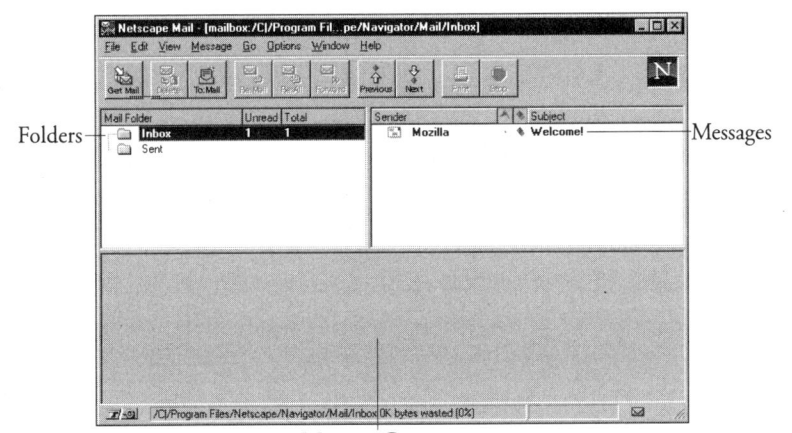

[Figure: Netscape Mail window with labels pointing to "Folders", "Messages", and "Message Contents"]

The Mail window is divided into three sections: folders, the list of messages in a selected folder, and the contents of a message. These sections are divided by movable bars. You might have to move the horizontal bar up in order to see all three.

The 10 buttons in the toolbar allow you to do the following:

	Get New Mail	Retrieve any new mail from the mail server.
	Delete	Move the current message to the Trash folder.
	Write New Mail	Compose and send a new message.
	Reply	Reply to the current message.
	Reply to All	Reply to the current message and send it to every recipient of the original message.
	Forward	Forward the current message to somebody.
	Previous	Read the previous unread message.
	Next	Read the next unread message.
	Print	Print the current message.
	Stop	Stop any current transfers.

The Inbox folder is currently selected. Netscapes stores all new messages in your Inbox folder.

2 In the **Messages** window, click the **Mozilla Welcome** message.

FIGURE 9.2

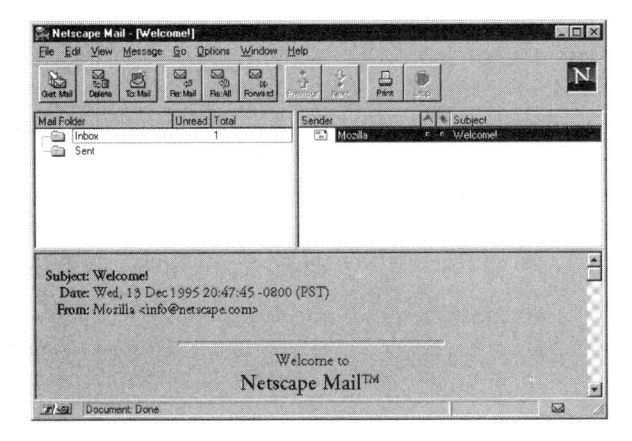

The message is selected and displayed.

3 Read the Mozilla message if you like. When you are finished with the message, click the second button from the left in the toolbar, **Delete Message**.

FIGURE 9.3

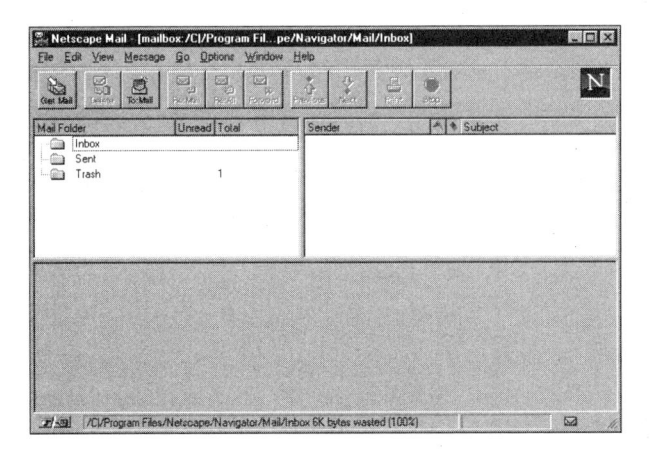

The message disappears and Netscape creates a new folder, Trash.

4 Click the Trash folder.

There's your message from Mozilla again. When you tell Netscape to delete a message, it second-guesses you and moves the message to the Trash folder. To truly delete messages, you would click File and click Empty Trash Folder.

> **tip** Be careful: Once you empty the trash, whatever was inside is gone forever.

You will add a name to your address book and send a message to that person. It is not necessary to enter someone in your address book before sending a message, but you will do so here so you know how to do both.

5 Click the **New Message** icon.

FIGURE 9.4

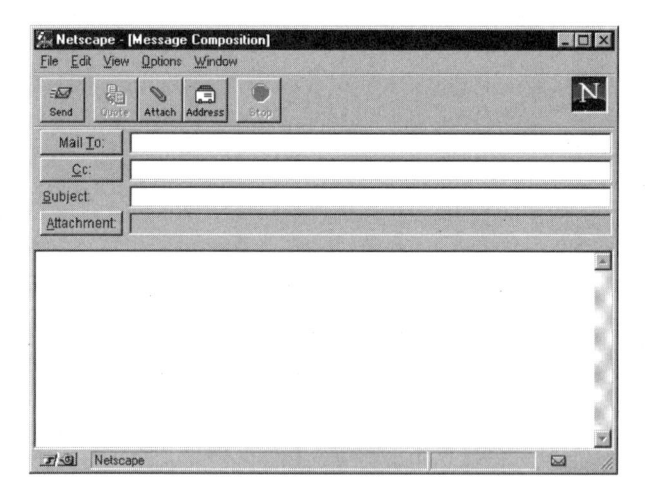

The Message Composition window opens. There are five buttons to aid you.

	Send	Sends the current message now.
	Quote	Puts the current message in quoted format.
	Attach	Attaches a file to send with the current message.
	Address	Opens the Address Book.
	Stop	Stops any current transfers.

6   Click **Window**. Click **Address Book**.

FIGURE 9.5

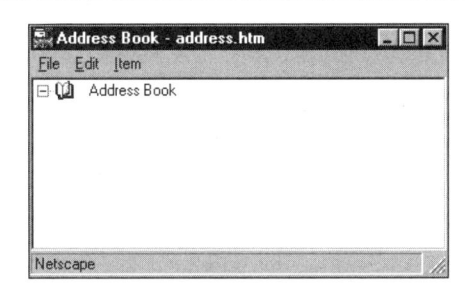

7   Click **Item**. Click **Add User**.

The Address Book Properties window opens.

As an exercise, you will send a message to your clone, who will then respond with a message that you can read in Chapter 11.

8   In the **Nickname** text box, type **clone**. In the **Name** text box, type **My Clone**. In the **E-Mail Address** text box, type your e-mail address. Click **OK**.

FIGURE 9.6

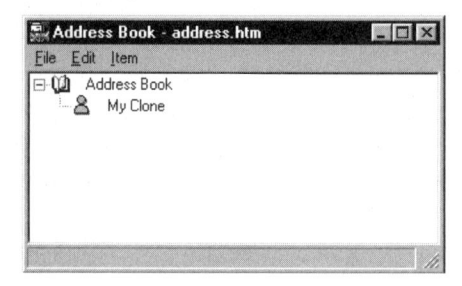

```
Address Book - address.htm
File  Edit  Item
─ Address Book
    └─ My Clone
```

You now have an entry in your Address Book for My Clone. You will next send a message to your clone, who will then send back an automatic reply so you can have something to receive in the exercise for reading e-mail.

9   In the Address Book window, click **File** and then click **Close**.

The Address Book closes. The Message Composition window should still be on top.

10   Click the **Mail To** button.

A list of your addresses opens.

11   Click **My Clone**. Click **To**. Click **OK**.

Note: If you did not want to enter this person into your Address Book, you could have typed the e-mail address directly into the Mail To text box.

You return to the Message Composition window. In the previous step, you clicked the To button to designate the recipient of the message.

My Clone appears in the To field.

> **tip** If you had several people in your Address Book and you wanted to send a message to more than one person, you would have clicked the first person, then clicked To, and finally clicked somebody else and CC (copy circulated).

12   Press **Tab** twice to get to the **Subject** field. Type **Hello**.

Notice that when you left the To field, Netscape filled in your clone's full address information.

13   Press **Tab** again to get to the message writing area. Type the following message:

> Dear Clone,
>
> I don't feel like working tomorrow.
> Could you please go to work for me,
> wash the car, mow the lawn, and take
> out the trash.
>
> Thanks. I'll be in the hot tub.
>
> Sincerely,
> Me

FIGURE 9.7

```
Netscape - [Message Composition]
File  Edit  View  Options  Window

Mail To:    My Clone <billder@fbeedle.com>
Cc:
Subject:    Hello
Attachment:

Dear Clone,

I don't feel like working tomorrow.
Could you please go to work for me,
wash the car, mow the lawn, and take
out the trash.

Thanks. I'll be in the hot tub.

Sincerely,
Me
```

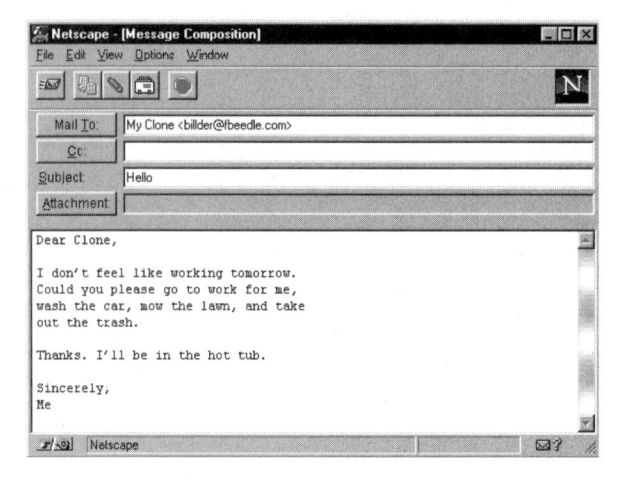

14   Click the **Send** icon.

Netscape logs onto your mail server, lights the Stop icon in case you change your mind fast, and mails your message. That's it! Your clone should reply shortly.

SENDING A FILE

To send a file via e-mail, you *attach* the file to an e-mail message. Navigator will attach the file to the end of your message when you send it.

15   Click the **New Message** icon.

Navigator opens the Message Composition window.

16   Click the **Attachment** button.

FIGURE 9.8

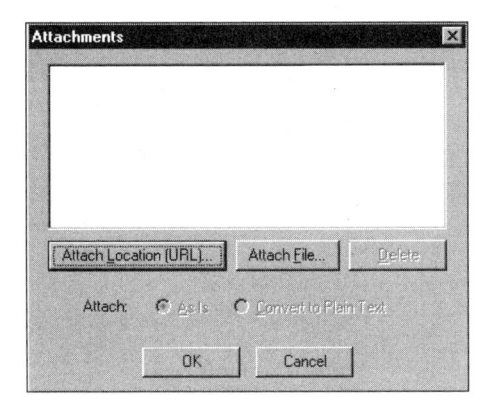

[Attachments dialog box screenshot]

The Attachment window opens.

17 Click **Attach Location (URL)**.

A dialog box appears. If you type a Web address here, a copy of the file at that address will be sent along with your message.

18 Click **Cancel**. Click **Attach File**.

Navigator displays a dialog box from which you can browse through your computer and select a file to attach. You will not send a file in this exercise.

19 Click **Cancel**. Click **Cancel**. Click **File**. Click **Close**. Click **Yes**.

E-Mail Links

Sometimes you will see Web pages with e-mail links. Clicking the link will leave Navigator's browser, open the Message Composition window, and insert the e-mail address into the To field.

20 Press **Alt + Tab** to return to the Navigator browser. Click the **Home** button.

CHAPTER 9   SENDING E-MAIL

You return to the Lunch Break Tutorial.

21   Click **Mail and News**.

This page displays a few links.

22   Hold the mouse pointer over the **E-mail the President** link and read the status bar.

You see the link says **mailto:president@whitehouse.gov**. The "mailto" signifies this link will send an e-mail address to the address shown.

23   Click **E-mail the President**.

FIGURE 9.9

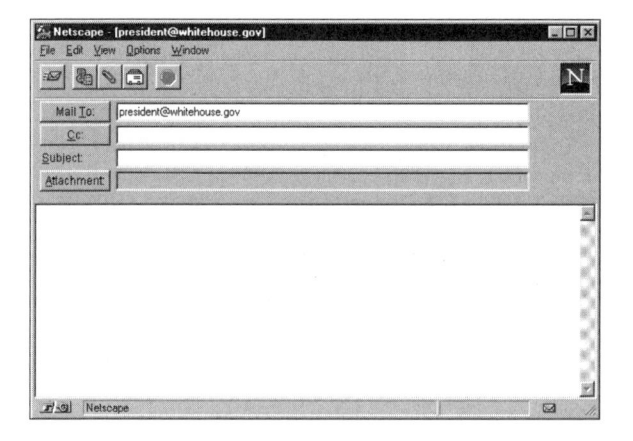

Navigator opens the Message Composition window. The To address is automatically filled. Go ahead and send a message if you like, but I wouldn't expect a personal reply any time soon.

By default, Netscape checks for mail every ten minutes. When it finds new mail for you, an exclamation point appears next to the envelope icon in the bottom right corner of the Netscape window. But instead of twiddling our thumbs waiting for mail, let's move on to Netscape News.

READING THE NEWS

Usenet is often compared to a coffeehouse with thousands of rooms. More accurately, it is an international collection of discussion groups on anything from vegetarian cooking (**rec.food.veg**) to the latest headline news (**misc.headlines**) to biomedical engineering (**sci.engr.biomed**).

No single organization controls Usenet. Newsgroups are distributed on *news servers* worldwide. When somebody posts an article to a newsgroup, every news server around the world that carries that newsgroup is sent a copy of the new article. Not every news server carries every newsgroup.

Access a newsgroup by *subscribing* to it (no charge, of course). After you've subscribed, you can read any articles that have been posted by other subscribers around the world. Read many articles within a newsgroup before posting your own article. Doing so will give you a feel for acceptable topics, as well as the tone of the discussion.

> **tip** Remember that posting an article sends it to computers worldwide, generating megabytes of data on the Internet backbone. It should not be taken lightly.

Understanding this section might be more difficult than previous ones, because this book can't guide you through a series of steps. In fact, it's impossible since the articles in newsgroups change daily. Remember that you are learning how to manuever in newsgroups, not to read the ones I am reading.

CHAPTER 10   READING THE NEWS

Note: Before you can perform these exercises, you must first configure Netscape to retrieve news properly. If you didn't do this in Chapter 9, please consult Appendix A, "Configuring Mail and News" before proceeding.

1   In Netscape's menu bar, click **Window**. Click **Netscape News**.

FIGURE 10.1

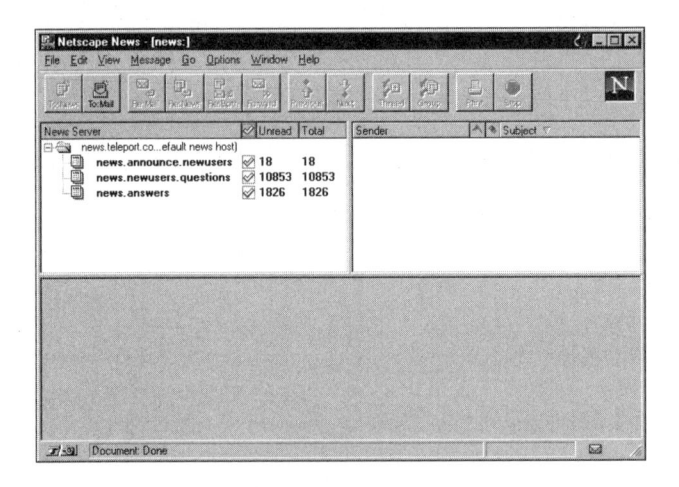

The Netscape News window appears. Netscape logs onto the news server (in this case, **news.teleport.com**) and loads three newsgroups to which new users are automatically subscribed. There are three panes in this window. The top left pane lists all newsgroups to which you are currently subscribed. The numbers to the right of the newsgroup names signify the number of unread articles in each newsgroup. The top right pane lists all the unread articles in the selected newsgroup. The large pane at the bottom displays your selected article. You will probably have these same newsgroups available.

Below the menu bar are 12 buttons. They are:

	Post New	Compose a new message and post it to a newsgroup.
	New Mail	Compose a new e-mail message.
	Mail Reply	Compose and e-mail a reply to the current message's author.
	Post Reply	Compose a reply to the current message and post it to a newsgroup.
	Post & Mail	Compose a reply to the current message, e-mail it to the message's author, and post it to a newsgroup.
	Forward	Forward the current message to somebody via e-mail.
	Previous	Read the previous unread message.
	Next	Read the next unread message.
	Thread Read	Mark messages in the current thread as read.
	All Read	Mark all messages in the current newsgroup as read.
	Print	Print the current message.
	Stop	Stop any current transfers.

CHAPTER 10   READING THE NEWS

2   Click **news.announce.newusers**. If you don't have this one, click one that sounds similar.

FIGURE 10.2

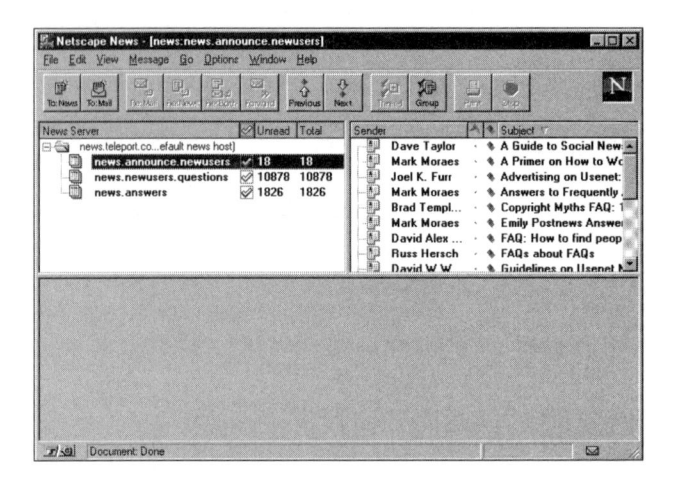

Netscape retrieves up to 100 articles in this newsgroup from the news server. (This amount can be changed in the Mail and News Preferences under the Options menu.) In this case, there are only 18 articles. There are two columns between the author's name and the subject of each article. A green mark in the second column signifies that the article is unread by you. The first column is for flagging articles you deem important.

3   Click in the title of the first article listed.

FIGURE 10.3

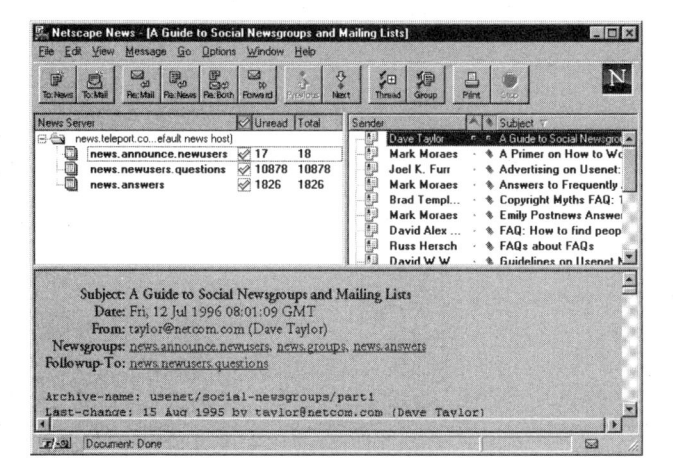

The article is displayed below. Notice the amount of unread articles listed next to the newsgroup is reduced by one. Notice also that the green mark next to the article's title disappeared, meaning that the article is no longer marked as unread. By default, Navigator retrieves articles that you have not read yet, so if you were to return to this newsgroup later this message would not be displayed. The other unread messages would be displayed, along with any other new messages.

4   Click the **Read Next Unread Message** button.

CHAPTER 10 READING THE NEWS

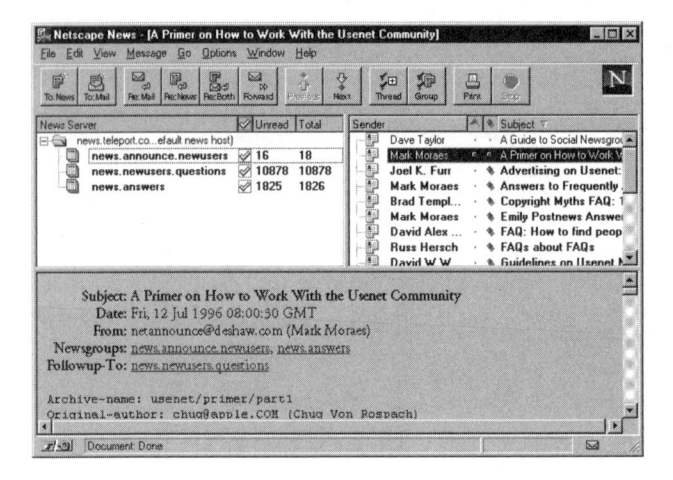

FIGURE 10.4

[Screenshot of Netscape News window showing "A Primer on How to Work With the Usenet Community"]

Netscape retrieves the next article unread by you. The counter of unread articles is again reduced by one and its unread marker is turned off. You can read through the article using the scroll bars.

> **tip** You should explore these "beginner's" newsgroups before you move on. They contain many informative articles about participating in Usenet newsgroups. Read them and learn the ways of the Usenet community from the masters. However, most of the Usenet teachings revolve around one central theme—treat people with respect.

When you have an article displayed, you can respond to that message in five ways. Post a reply to the message to the entire newsgroup. E-mail a reply to the message's author. Post a reply to the entire newsgroup *and* e-mail your reply to the message's author. Forward a copy of the current message to somebody else. In this exercise, we will do the last—read it and move on. Later, if you wish, you can respond to an article.

> *tip* First, remember to read many articles in your chosen newsgroup because somebody else may have already addressed your question. Second, remember that your posting will be read by thousands of people, so write with care.

You will quickly become bored with these three newsgroups, and you will want to access the thousands of others. Suppose you are tracing the history of your family and you hear of a great newsgroup at **soc.genealogy.surnames**. You need to open this newsgroup.

5   Click **File**. Click **Add Newsgroup**.

A dialog box asks you which newsgroup you want to open.

6   Type **soc.genealogy.surnames**

FIGURE 10.5

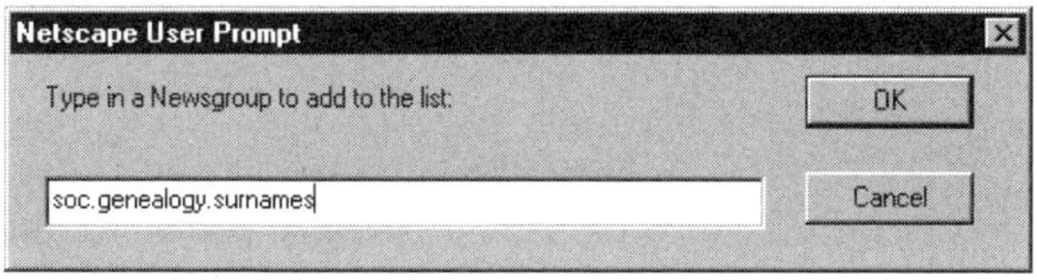

7   Click **OK**, and wait.

CHAPTER 10   READING THE NEWS

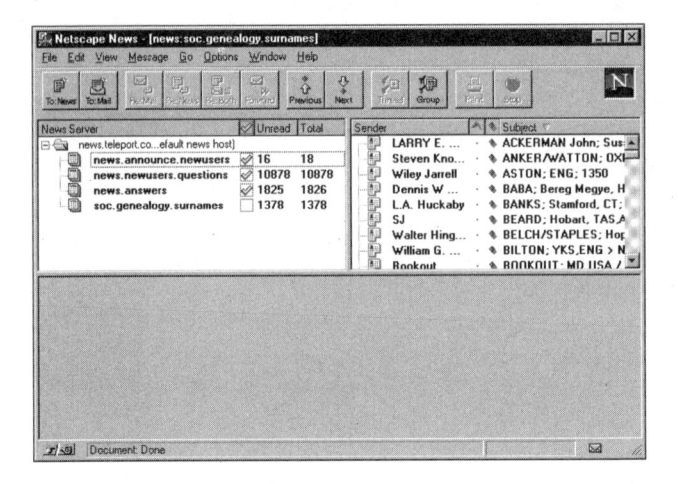

FIGURE 10.6

[screenshot of Netscape News window showing news:soc.genealogy.surnames]

Netscape added the newsgroup **soc.genealogy.surnames** to your list and downloaded the first 100 articles. You still need to subscribe to it so that the next time you access Netscape News, that newsgroup will appear.

8 Click in the empty box to the right of **soc.genealogy.surnames**, in the column of yellow checkmarks.

The checkmark signifies that you are now subscribed to this newsgroup. Suppose that you found nothing interesting in the first 100 messages and want to search through more.

9 Click **File**. Click **Get More Messages**.

Netscape retrieves the next 100 messages.

> **tip** Sometimes you will see Web pages with links to newsgroups. Clicking the link will leave Navigator's browser, open the News window, and display the newsgroup.

NETSCAPE ON YOUR LUNCH BREAK

10 Return to the Navigator browser. Click the **Home** button.

You return to the Lunch Break Tutorial.

11 Click **Mail and News**.

This page displays a few links.

12 Click the **rec.sport.table-tennis** newsgroup.

FIGURE 10.7

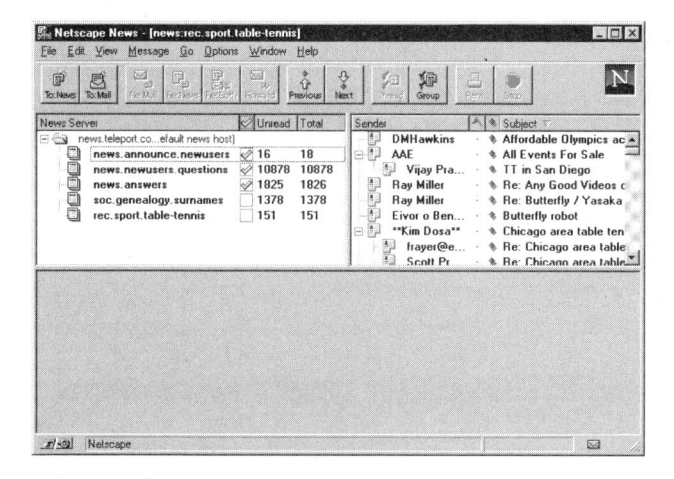

There is more than one way to access newsgroups. Navigator returns to the News window and opens the **rec.sport.table-tennis** newsgroup.

Thousands of Usenet newsgroups are available to you. If you want to retrieve the entire list of newsgroups available on your news server, click Options and then click Show All Newsgroups. Be warned, this list will be large and take several minutes to download. Subscribe to any newsgroups that sound interesting and have fun!

13 When you are finished with the News, click **File**. Click **Close**.

75

Reading E-Mail

During the previous exercise, an exclamation point may have appeared next to the envelope icon. If so, you have mail! (If not, return to this exercise when an exclamation point appears.)

If you have received mail...

1   Click the envelope icon.

FIGURE 11.1

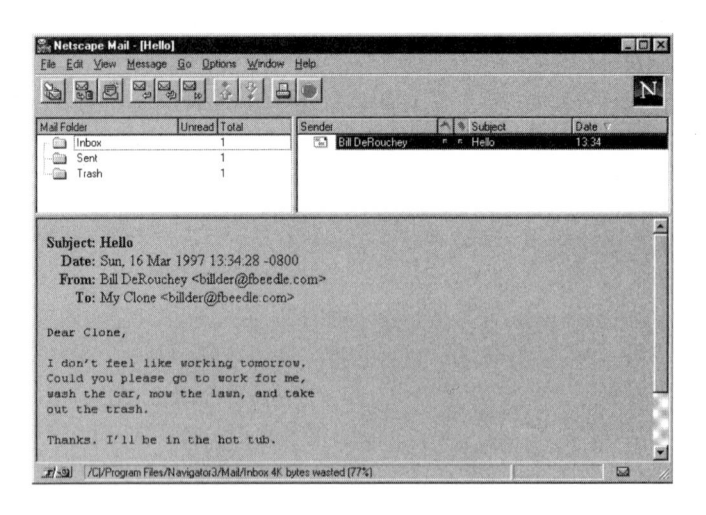

The Netscape Mail window appears. In the status bar at the bottom of the window, Navigator tells you how many messages it is currently downloading. Navigator automatically displays the Inbox and opens your first new message.

There is your message from your clone. Navigator also saves every piece of mail you send.

2 Click the **Sent** folder.

There is the message you sent to your clone. Navigator saves all your outgoing and incoming mail. This could become a big mess. That's why Netscape Mail provides folders.

3 Click **File**. Click **New Folder**.

FIGURE 11.2

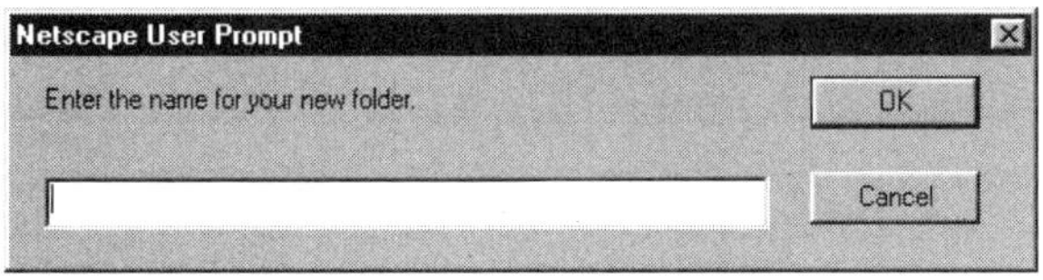

4 In the dialog box, type **My Clone** and click **OK**.

A new folder, My Clone, is created.

5 With the **Sent** folder still selected, drag your original message into the **My Clone** folder.

6 Click the **Inbox** folder. Drag your clone's reply into the **My Clone** folder.

7 Click the **My Clone** folder.

CHAPTER 11   READING E-MAIL

FIGURE 11.3

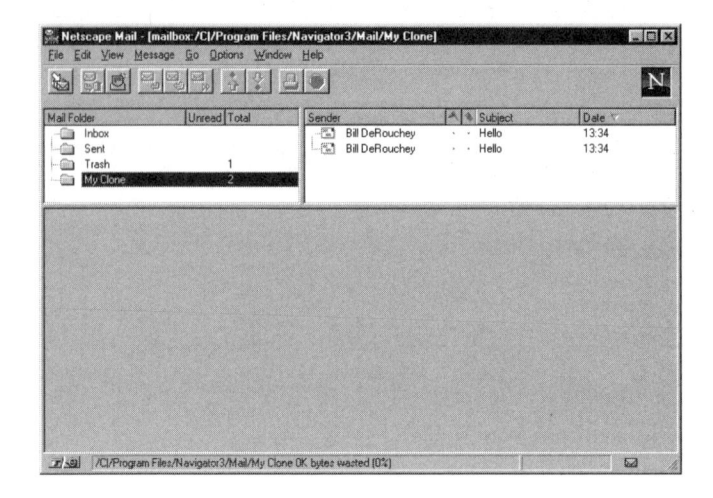

Both your original message and your clone's reply are neatly organized in the My Clone folder.

8   Click **File**. Click **Close**.

FRAMES

Netscape introduced frames to the World Wide Web. This innovation further distanced Navigator from its competitors. However, version 3.0 of Microsoft's Internet Explorer has adopted frames, potentially solidifying frames on the Web.

Normally when navigating the Web, you only see one page at a time. Frames allow you to see multiple pages by dividing the viewing area into several windows called, you guessed it, frames. Each frame contains one page of anything—text, graphics, sounds, whatever.

The most common use of frames is to provide a stationary toolbar that sits in a thin frame along one of the four edges of the page. Links for a site's main sections are placed in this toolbar frame. Clicking any of these links can then instruct the large remaining frame to retrieve a new page. The toolbar frame is the master and the remaining frame is the slave.

Confused? Think back to the Mail and News windows. Clicking a selection in the top left frame altered the top right frame. Clicking a selection in the top right frame altered the bottom frame. This is exactly how frames operate, except in this case, the author of the site defines the frames' size, position, and hierarchy.

CHAPTER 12   FRAMES

1   Click the **Home** button.

You return to the Lunch Break Tutorial.

2   Click **Frames**.

FIGURE 12.1

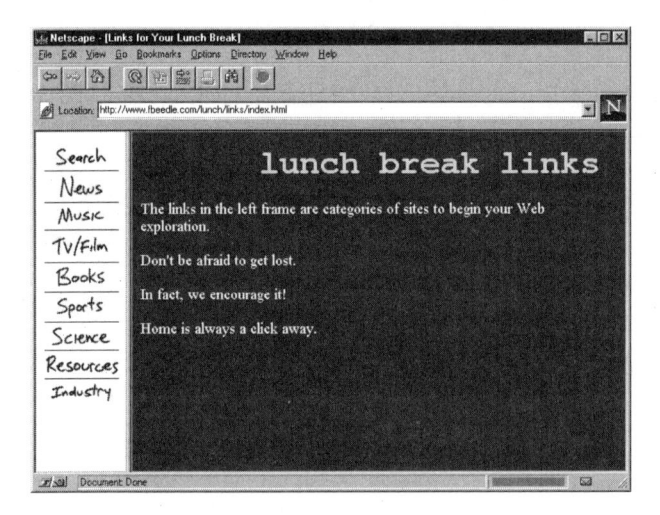

You arrive at a collection of links. The window is divided into two frames—a thin one to the left and a larger one to the right. The thin frame contains several topics to choose from. Even though they might not look like it, they are buttons. Whenever you see a list organized like this, the listed topics will usually be active links that you can choose from. Clicking a button in the thin frame will change the large frame.

3   In the thin frame, click **TV/Film**. Click **Resources**. Click **News**.

FIGURE 12.2

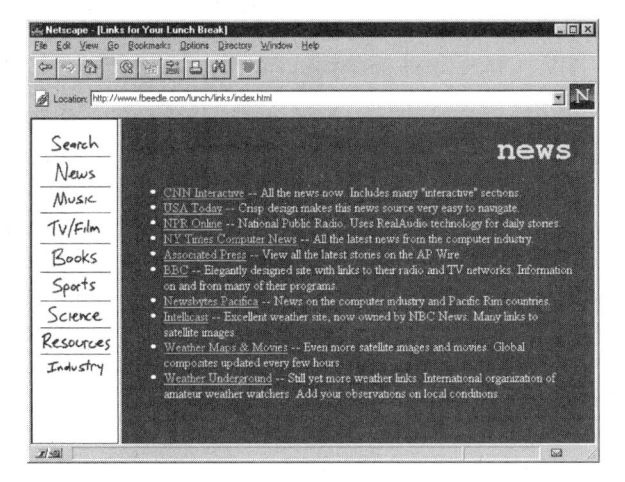

The thin frame controls the large frame. Each click in the thin frame changes the contents of the large frame. Notice that the thin frame remains unchanged. News links are currently displayed.

4 In the large frame, click **CNN**.

FIGURE 12.3

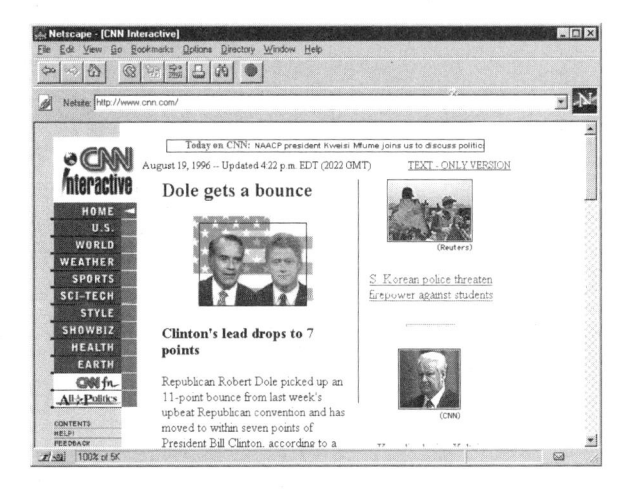

CHAPTER 12   FRAMES

Both frames disappear and the entire window is replaced by CNN. If created correctly, frames will disappear at the appropriate time. The frames only operate within the site called "Lunch Break Links."

5   In Navigator's toolbar, click the **Back** button.

You return to the News page of the framed Links site. Navigator remembered where you were within the framed site. The Back button works differently in Navigator versions 2 and 3. In version 2, clicking the Back button within a framed site would take you to the last page *outside* the framed site. This would be the last page you visited before entering the framed site. To move back within a framed site, you have to click the right mouse button and click Back. In version 3, the navigation of the Back button is more intuitive. Clicking the Back button takes you to the last page you saw, whether within frames or not.

6   (for version 3 users) In Navigator's toolbar, click the **Back** button.

6   (for version 2 users) Click the right mouse button. Click **Back**.

You arrive at the Resources page, the last page you visited before the News page. This is a listing of nifty things you might need on the Web, such as plug-ins and utilities.

That's it for frames!

13

MULTIMEDIA ON THE WEB

The Web boomed once it was transformed from a text-only to a graphical environment. Seemingly overnight, millions of people downloaded Mosaic, and then Netscape Navigator, to "surf" and "cruise" the Web. The next wave is now in motion: video, live audio, animated pages. In short, multimedia is taking over the Web. Some of it is still obscure and clunky, but in the rapid pace of Web development, these new capabilities will be smooth and easy before you can blink an eye.

Interactivity is the foundation of the next developmental wave of the Web. Users crave to do more than just look at nice pages with interesting information. They want to participate, to interact, to talk to people. Chat rooms are amazingly popular, as are multiplayer online games.

The biggest developments are Java, live audio and video, Shockwave, and VRML. This chapter will explain each in turn and guide you to the tools necessary to use them. Links to all sites mentioned herein are available on the Lunch Break Tutorial site. To access this, click the Home button to access the site, and then click Multimedia.

JAVA

The big buzzword in the online world is *Java*, a programming language for creating Internet applications. According to its creators at Sun Microsystems, "Java is a simple, robust, object-oriented, platform-independent, multi-threaded, dynamic general-purpose programming environment." That's a mouthful.

To best understand Java, we need to dig into its roots, when it was still known as Oak and the Web was just a remote, untapped corner of the Internet. Oak was initially developed as a universal communications language for consumer electronics, allowing TVs to talk with VCRs, alarm systems with telephones, toasters with light switches, and so on. Oak would accomplish this as a language independent of, yet simple to interpret into, the varying machine languages of each device.

At the time, interactive TV was the big future hype and Sun focused Oak upon the set-top boxes that would bring you the fabled 500 channels of programming. This is still hype; consequently, Oak withered. But when the Web exploded in the computer industry, Sun retooled Oak for Web applications and renamed it Java.

Java allows programmers to create software applets that can run on any computer. The implications of this are huge. Most computers, excluding extreme examples, use only one operating system. They are either a Windows system or a Macintosh or a UNIX, and so on. You acquire software designed for your particular system. This forces programmers to create versions of their software for each differing system. But with Java, this logjam could disappear. Programs written in Java are platform-independent, so it doesn't matter what platform they run on as long as the platform is Java-enabled, as most are.

Java is still young, but you can view examples of it on the Web. The primary site for collecting Java applets is Gamelan, located at **http://www.gamelan.com/**. Gamelan has examples ranging from business to games to education. This site can be accessed from the Lunch Break Tutorial. Figure 13.1 shows an image from JavaGammon, a site where you can play backgammon and chat with an opponent. Granted, playing backgammon live isn't earth-shattering, but it does provide a glimpse into the possibilities of interactivity over the Web.

FIGURE 13.1

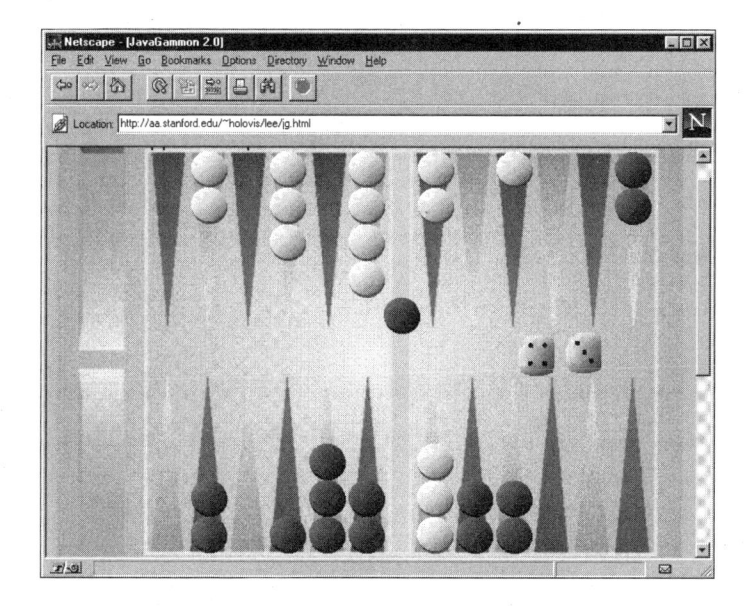

Live Audio and Video

Audio files are huge and video files are worse. These files take far more time to download than it does to watch or listen to them. Some day, modems will be fast enough and Internet lines will be fat enough that this won't be a problem. Until then, the solution is to stream audio and video files.

Streaming is playing the file while it downloads. The sound file is downloaded and seamlessly played a chunk at a time. RealAudio, developed by Progressive Networks, was the pioneer of streaming audio. It requires at least a 14.4 modem to work effectively. Now in version 3, RealAudio sites are popping up everywhere. You can hear recorded stories broadcast on NPR or ABC. You can listen to any of the dozens of radio stations broadcasting live on the Internet. You can also listen to live sports broadcasts. The sound quality is often reminiscent of AM radio, but at this early stage, so what! It will get better, faster, and eventually as common as plain old radio.

When you access a RealAudio file, the RealAudio player opens. It contains Play, Pause, and Stop buttons, as well as a volume control on the right.

Figure 13.2

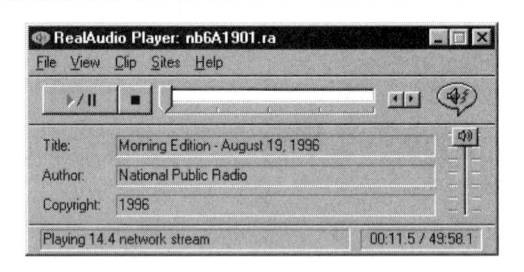

Streaming video is the next step after streaming audio. At this writing, several companies offer streaming plug-ins but none have emerged as the front runner. But like most things on the Web, wait a few months and streaming video will be common. A year, and it'll be ubiquitous.

Shockwave

Shockwave is pure multimedia, a combination of animation, sound, video, graphics, and text. For years, the standard in creating multimedia has been Macromedia Director. Many of the multimedia CD-ROM titles available were created in Director. Now, Director files can be placed on the Web by being compressed into the Shockwave format.

Shockwave has generated a lot of excitement because it is easier to create simple animations in Director than via a full programming language such as Java. Figure 13.3 shows an example from the Rainforest Action Network. The bulldozer moves across the screen, chomping down the rainforest.

FIGURE 13.3

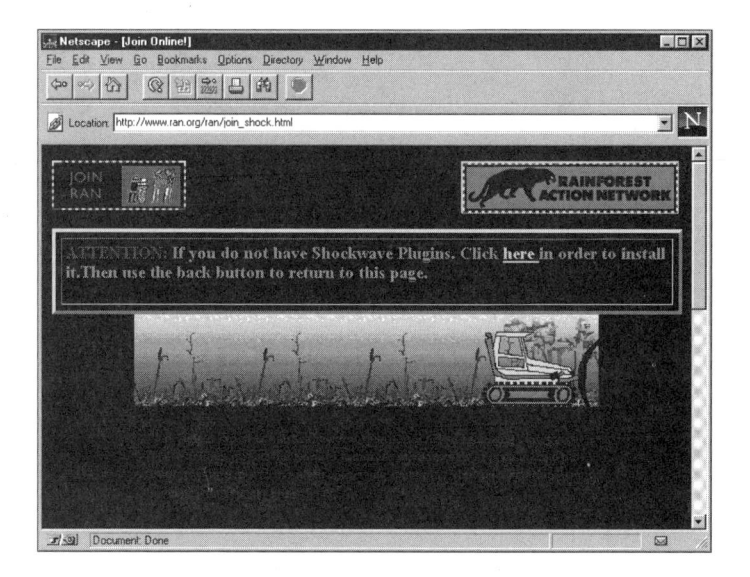

Shockwave is also useful for children's games. Figure 13.4 shows a Shockwave page from Disney's version of Roald Dahl's *James and the Giant Peach*. Here you can build your own bug by moving around the body parts while listening to a soundtrack of crickets and frogs.

FIGURE 13.4

VRML

VRML stands for *Virtual Reality Modeling Language*. Much as HTML uses a text file to describe a page with graphics, VRML describes a 3-D virtual world using only text. Navigator includes a plug-in called Live3D that interprets the VRML text into the 3-D world that you see.

Virtual reality has myriad uses, whether modeling existing scenes, creating new worlds, or providing a visual representation of scientific data. For example, Figure 13.5 is from Virtual San Diego.

FIGURE 13.5

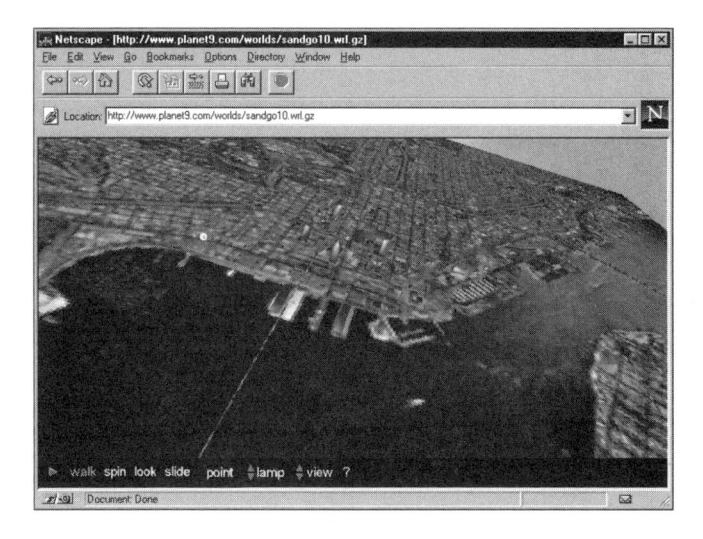

VRML can also be a pure art form in itself. Figure 13.6 is by Mark Pesce, the creator of VRML.

FIGURE 13.6

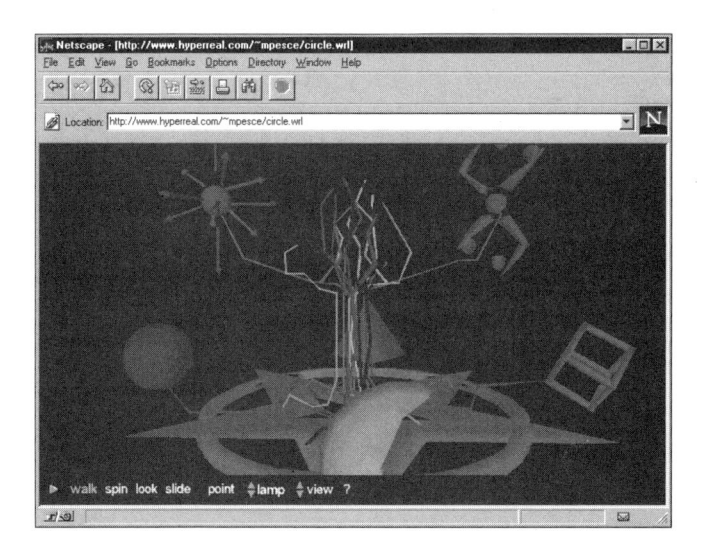

A

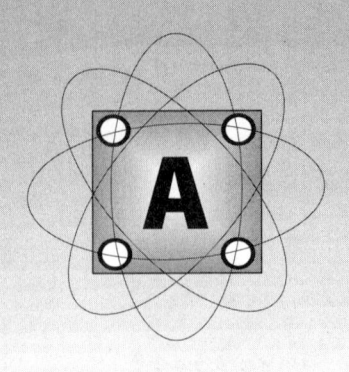

CONFIGURING MAIL AND NEWS

Netscape accesses e-mail and Usenet newsgroups from the server that is located at your Internet provider. Therefore, you must first tell Netscape where to find them before you can use either Netscape News or Netscape Mail.

1   Click **Options**. Click **Mail and News Preferences**.

The Preferences dialog box opens, displaying five organizational tabs: Appearance, Composition, Servers, Identity, and Organization. Each section in the Preferences represents an area of Netscape that you can customize. For this exercise, we are only concerned with Servers and Identity.

2   Click the **Identity** tab.

This section lets Netscape know who you are so it can automatically supply this information in your e-mail and news articles.

3   In the **Your Name** text box, type your name as you wish it to appear.

4   In the **Your Email** text box, type your e-mail address.

5   In the **Reply-to Address** text box, again type your e-mail address.

Your screen should resemble Figure A.1 except for your specific information.

FIGURE A.1

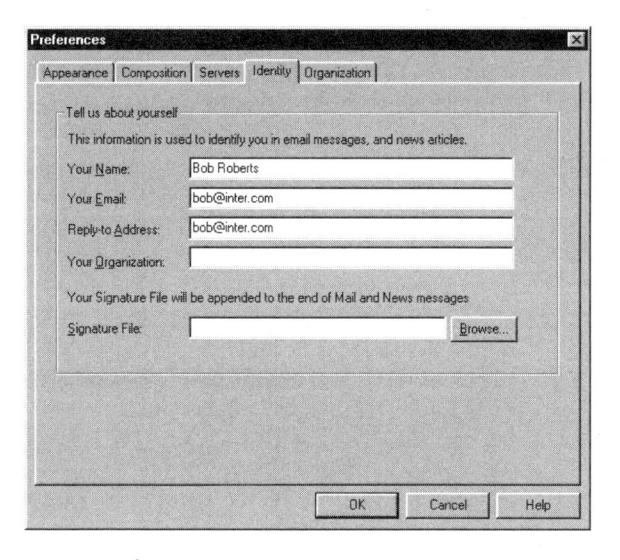

That's all for Identity.

6   Click the **Servers** tab.

> **tip** Not every Internet provider uses the same naming conventions, although the ones used here are the most common. If they do not work, you will need to contact your Internet provider and ask them what the names are for the mail server and the news server.

Most Internet providers just add **mail** or **news** before their name when naming these servers. Try this first. I will use the fictitious name **whatever.com**. Substitute your provider's name there. Don't forget to include the periods between **mail** (or **news**) and **whatever.com**.

APPENDIX A   CONFIGURING MAIL AND NEWS

7   In the **Outgoing Mail (SMTP) Server** text box, type **mail.whatever.com**.

8   In the **Incoming Mail (POP3) Server** text box, type **mail.whatever.com**.

9   In the **POP3 User Name** text box, type your user name only. Do *not* add *@whatever.com*.

10 In the **News (NNTP) Server** text box, type **news.whatever.com**.

Your screen should resemble Figure A.2 except for your specific information:

FIGURE A.2

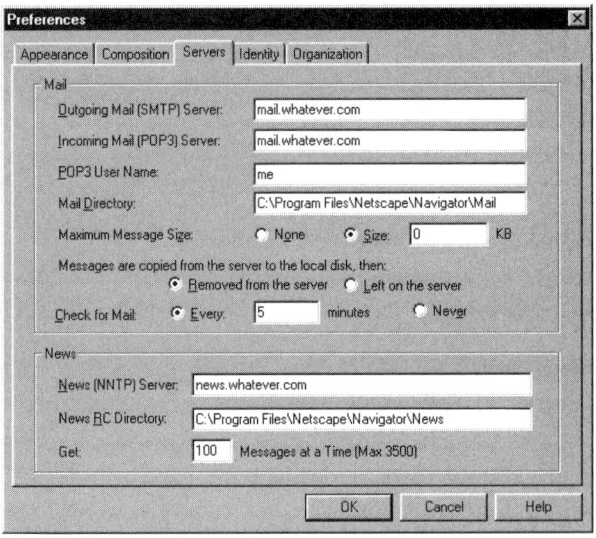

11 Click **OK**.

That's all. You should now be able to access e-mail and Usenet newsgroups. Again, if these names do not seem to work, please contact your Internet provider to find out the correct ones.

PLUG-INS

Plug-ins are programs that extend the normal functionality of Navigator. They play audio or video clips, display 3-D VRML worlds, or provide other similar multimedia possibilities. You have already read about a few plug-ins in Chapter 13, such as RealAudio and Shockwave.

Each time Navigator encounters a file, it determines how to handle the file depending on the file's extension and the MIME type. The *MIME type* is a file description attached to the file by the server so that browsers such as Navigator know what to expect. By itself, Navigator can only display the following file types: HTM and HTML files are Web pages; GIF and JPG (or JPEG) are the two basic graphic types; and TXT is a plain text file. Beyond these, Navigator consults its inner list to determine which, if any, plug-in to use to display the file.

For example, suppose you click a link to load a RealAudio file. You know from the context of the page that it is a RealAudio file, but Navigator doesn't. Once it retrieves the file, it notices that its file extension is RA and its MIME type is "audio/x-pn-realaudio." Navigator opens the RealAudio player and plays the file.

Other Plug-ins

QuickTime (QT, MOV)—Apple's movie format. The QuickTime for Windows player can be downloaded from Apple at **http://quicktime.apple.com/**. Also interesting is QuickTime Virtual Reality, a movie in which you can move around the camera lens and view the full range of vision. The QuickTime VR player can be downloaded from Apple at **http://qtvr.quicktime.apple.com/**.

Adobe Acrobat Reader (PDF)—Adobe Acrobat's Portable Document Format. This allows a page to be viewed exactly as it was created in a program such as Adobe PageMaker or Microsoft Word. It is available from Adobe at **http://www.adobe.com**.

Configuring a Plug-In

Most plug-ins configure themselves when you install them, but not all do. Occasionally, you may need to configure a plug-in yourself. Do not perform the steps now, but read along so that you will understand how to configure a plug-in. This exercise will use RealAudio as an example. Suppose that its documentation tells you that the RealAudio MIME type is "audio/x-pn-realaudio."

1   Click **Options**. Click **General Preferences**. If it is not already selected, click the **Helpers** tab.

FIGURE B.1

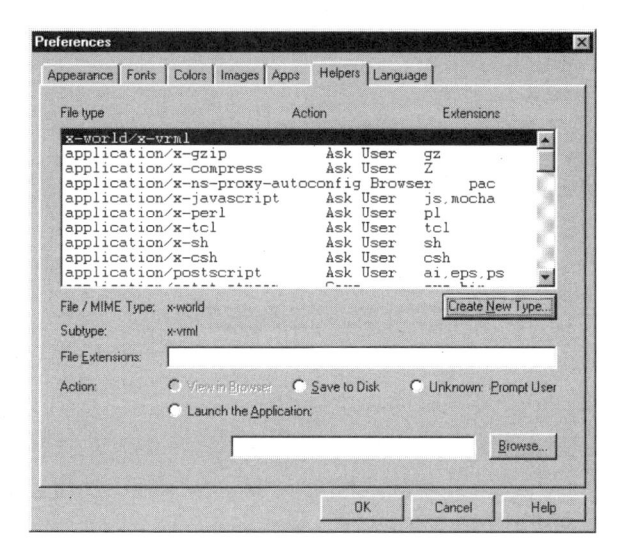

The Preferences dialog box Helpers tab displays a list of MIME file types. The Action column tells Navigator how to handle the corresponding file extension in the Extensions column. "Browser" in the Action column tells Navigator to display the file directly in Navigator's content window. "Ask User" prompts Navigator to ask the user what to do with the file. "Save" tells Navigator to open a Save As dialog box.

2   Click **Add New Type**.

FIGURE B.2

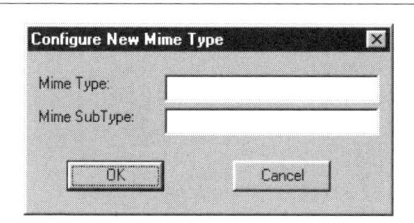

APPENDIX B   PLUG-INS

A dialog box opens in which you enter the MIME type and MIME subtype. The type precedes the forward slash and the subtype follows it. In our example of "audio/x-pn-realaudio," the MIME type is "audio" and the subtype is "x-pn-realaudio."

3   In the **Mime Type** text box, type **audio**

4   In the **Mime SubType** text box, type **x-pn-realaudio**

FIGURE B.3

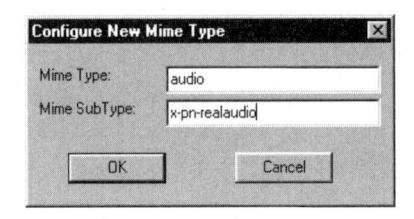

5   Click **OK**.

A new file type is added to the list and displayed. You can now specify which file extensions will trigger your new plug-in. In this case, RealAudio files use either RA or RAM for a file extension.

6   In the **File Extensions** text box, type **RA, RAM**

One last step. You need to tell Navigator where the RealAudio player is located on your computer. Suppose that it is located at C:\RealAudio\Raplayer.exe.

7   Click the **Launch the Application** radio button. In the text box below it, type **C:\RealAudio\Raplayer.exe**

> tip: You could also have clicked Browse to search through your directories to find the file.

8   Click **OK**.

You have closed the Preferences dialog box and saved your changes.

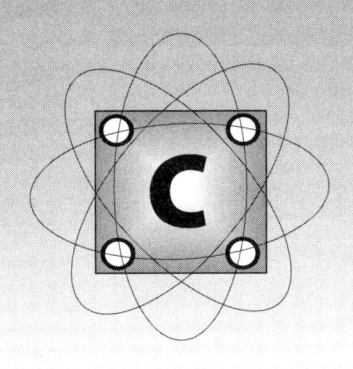

Netscape 3.0 Menu Options

File

New Web Browser Opens a new copy of the Netscape Navigator browser.

New Mail Message Opens the Mail Composition window for writing e-mail.

Mail Document Sends a copy of the current page to anybody via e-mail.

Open Location Opens a page on the Web.

Open File Opens a page from the local computer.

Save As Saves the current page to the local computer.

Page Setup Prepares the current page for printing.

Print Prints the current page.

Print Preview Displays how the current page will look when printed.

Close Closes the current window.

Exit Quits Netscape and closes all windows.

EDIT

Undo Reverses effects from the last command.

Cut Removes any highlighted text and places it on the Clipboard.

Copy Places a copy of any highlighted text on the Clipboard.

Paste Inserts the contents of the Clipboard into the current cursor position.

Select All Highlights the entire current document for copying or cutting.

Find Searches for a word(s) in the current document.

Find Again Repeats the last Find command.

VIEW

Reload Reloads the current page from the Web or local disk.

Reload Frame In Web sites using frames, reloads a single frame.

Load Images Loads images for the current page, assuming that Auto Load Images (Options menu) is unchecked.

Refresh Redisplays the current page.

Document Source Displays the HTML source code for the current page.

Document Info Displays basic information about the current page.

Frame Source Displays the HTML source code for a single frame.

Frame Info Displays basic information about a single frame.

Go

Back Returns to the previous page in the History List, if possible.

Forward Jumps to the next page in the History List, if possible.

Home Loads the default home page.

Stop Loading Halts loading of the current page.

0 Home Page The History List. After a typical Netscape session, this list will have over 20 entries.

Bookmarks

Add Bookmark Creates a bookmark for the current page.

Go to Bookmarks Displays the entire Bookmark List.

Options

General Preferences Adjusts colors and fonts. Installs helper applications. Defines your home page.

Mail and News Preferences Configures Netscape Mail and Netscape News.

Network Preferences Adjusts your disk and memory caches.

Security Preferences Configures security options.

Show Toolbar Shows/hides the toolbar: Back, Forward, Home, etc.

Show Location Shows/hides the Location text box.

Show Directory Buttons Shows/hides the What's New, What's Cool, etc. buttons.

Show Java Console Shows a window detailing any Java activity.

Auto Load Images Defines whether images are automatically loaded.

Document Encoding Chooses which language you wish to work in.

DIRECTORY

Netscape's Home Jumps to the Netscape Corporation's home page.

What's New! Displays what's new on the Web, according to Netscape.

What's Cool! Displays what's cool on the Web, according to Netscape.

Netscape Galleria A list of companies using Netscape's server software.

Netscape Destinations A categorized selection of Internet features.

Internet Search View Netscape's collection of Web search engines.

People View Netscape's links to "phone books" of e-mail addresses.

About the Internet Netscape's general introduction to the Internet.

WINDOW

Netscape Mail Opens Netscape Mail to send or receive e-mail.

Netscape News Opens Netscape News to access Usenet newsgroups.

Address Book Opens your e-mail Address Book.

Bookmarks Opens your list of bookmarks.

History Displays your History List.

0 Netscape Home Page The list of open windows. If you also opened Netscape Mail and Netscape News, there would be three listings here.

Help

About Netscape Displays information about your copy of Netscape Navigator.

About Plug-ins Displays information about plug-ins, helper applications.

Registration Information Registers your copy of Netscape Navigator online.

Software Displays software available at Netscape.

Handbook Accesses tutorials on Netscape.

Release Notes Displays information about your version of Netscape Navigator.

Frequently Asked Questions Answers the most common questions about Netscape.

On Security Discusses security on the Internet.

How to Give Feedback Reports errors, praise.

How to Get Support Technical support.

How to Create Web Services Discusses how to create your own Web pages.

GLOSSARY

Address A specific location on the Internet. *See also* URL.

Applet A small application created with Java and designed for the Web.

Article A message posted to a Usenet newsgroup.

Cache Where Netscape temporarily stores all downloaded files. Typically this is the directory c:\netscape\cache. When you instruct Netscape to access a page, it first checks the cache to see if a copy of that page, or any graphics on it, are stored in your cache. If so, it retrieves the local version first to save access time.

Domain name The name of a specific computer on the Internet, such as www.bigcomputer.com.

E-mail Electronic mail. You can send messages to anybody with an e-mail address. It works similar to the traditional postal service, only much faster.

Form An interactive HTML page, usually including text boxes, radio buttons, drop-down lists, and command buttons. By entering information into the form and clicking a Submit button, you can receive information specific to your request. A common example is a search engine.

Frames A feature introduced with Netscape 2.0. The content area is divided into sections, each of which displays a different Web page. For example, one frame can contain the Web site's toolbar while another displays its information. Clicking the first frame can cause the second frame to change its display while the first frame stays the same.

Helper application A software application loaded by Netscape to display a file that Netscape cannot display by itself. Common examples are helper applications that will play movies or sound clips.

Hit 1. A successful match when searching a database. 2. When someone accesses a Web page. Used for counting purposes, e.g. "My page received over one million hits today."

Home page The initial page seen when jumping to a Web site, akin to the foyer in a building.

HTML Hypertext Markup Language. The language in which Web pages are written. The ease of writing HTML files sparked the popularity of publishing on the Web.

Internet A community of people who share information via a worldwide collection of computers connected using phone lines, high-speed data cables, and satellites.

Internet service provider A company that provides Internet accounts. Usually, you pay a monthly fee for a certain amount of hours of Internet access.

Java A language designed for the Internet and developed by Sun Corporation.

JavaScript A scripting language for creating small routines within Web pages.

Link A jump from one page to another. Most Web pages contain portions of text or graphics that, when clicked, tell the Web browser to leave the current page and load a new one. Text links appear different from regular text; they are usually blue and/or underlined. Graphic links often look similar to buttons. Jumping from link to link is the hypertext in HTTP.

Mail server A computer that processes e-mail. All e-mail is stored on the mail server until the user retrieves it.

News server A computer that processes Usenet newsgroups. The news server collects articles that are posted to the newsgroups and stores them for users to read.

Page One file viewed on the World Wide Web. "Loading a page" is simply accessing a file somewhere on the Web. Also called Web page.

Plug-in Software that enchances Navigator's normal functionality, such as audio players, video players, or other multimedia enhancements.

Post To send an article to a Usenet newsgroup.

Protocol A method of transferring data over the Internet or any network. Computers on both the sending and receiving ends of a transfer need to speak the same language in order to transfer data. Examples include FTP (File Transfer Protocol), Gopher, and HTTP (Hypertext Transfer Protocol).

Glossary

Search engine A Web site that functions as a large searchable database of other locations on the Internet. You use a search engine to search for any instances on the Web of the keyword(s) you are interested in.

Shockwave A multimedia file type created in one of Macromedia's software applications—Director, Authorware, or Freehand.

Subscribe To join a Usenet newsgroup.

Substring A portion of text that is contained within a longer chunk of text. For example, "the" is a substring of "other." Substrings are often used in searching. For example, searching for "zoolog" will also find "zoology" and "zoological."

Thread A topic of discussion in a Usenet newsgroup. As people reply to previous replies to an original message, a thread develops like a long chain or train of messages.

URL Uniform Resource Locator. An Internet designation that describes a location of a file or a computer within the Internet.

Usenet A collection of discussion groups (newsgroups) on most topics. People contribute to newsgroups by posting new articles or replying to other ones.

VRML Virtual Reality Modeling Language. A language with which you can describe a complex virtual reality world with a simple text file.

Web browser Software for viewing the World Wide Web. Examples include Netscape, Mosaic, and Internet Explorer.

Web site A collection of Web pages. The relationship between Web pages and a Web site is similar to rooms in a house. In a house, each room is a separate entity, yet collectively they define the house. You can move from the kitchen to the dining room to the living room. In a Web site, you can jump from page to page, yet the sum of these pages defines the Web site.

World Wide Web A portion of the Internet that uses HTTP to transfer graphics, sound, and movies in addition to plain text. Currently the most popular section of the Internet.

INDEX

A–D
addresses, 10, 27–28
AltaVista, 35, 39
Andreessen, Marc, 2
audio, 86
bookmark, 8, 9
   creating, 32–34
   organizing, 43–48
Clark, Jim, 2
copyrights, 42
domain names, 28–29
   country codes, 29
   suffixes, 29

E
e-mail, 56–64
   Address Book, 61–63
   buttons, 58
   configuring, 90–92
   file sending, 64–65
   links, 65–66
   Message Composition window, 61
   reading, 76–78
   Trash, 60
error messages, 49–53

F–H
File Transfer Protocol (FTP), 27
forms, 36
frames, 79–82
gopher, 27
home page
   changing, 25–26
Hypertext Markup Language (HTML), 30
hypertext transfer protocol (HTTP), 27

I–M
infobots, 39
Internet Protocol address (IP address), 28
Java, 1, 84–85
links, 8–10
Lycos, 35, 39
Macromedia Director, 87
multimedia, 84

N
Netscape Navigator
   content area, 6
   directory buttons, 5
   History, 15–16
   home page, 3, 8
   launching, 3
   Location field, 5, 9, 10
   Mail icons, 6
   menu bar, 4
   navigation buttons, 9
   Progress bar, 7
   screen
      customizing, 23–25

Scroll bars, 6
Security Indicator, 7
Status Message area, 7
Title Bar, 4
Toolbar, 5
    Back and Forward, 14
    Find, 16–17
    Home, 22
    Images, 18–21
    Open, 22
    Print, 22
    Show Directory, 23
    using, 13–22
Netscape Navigator 3.0 menu options
    Bookmarks, 99
    Directory, 100
    Edit, 98
    File, 97
    Go, 99
    Help, 101
    Options, 99
    View, 98
    Window, 100
newsgroups, 67–75
    adding, 73
    menu bar, 69
    reading, 70–72
    subscribing, 67
news reader
    configuring, 91–94
news servers, 67

P–R

plug–ins, 93–96
    configuring, 94–96
protocol, 2
RealAudio, 86
robots, 39

S–T

saving, 24
search engine, 35
searching, 35–42
    hit, 35
    match, 35
Shockwave, 1, 87
shortcuts, 55
spiders, 39
streaming, 86
troubleshooting
    emptying cache, 53–54
tilde (~), 28

U–Y

Uniform Resource Locator (URL), 5, 27
Usenet, 1
video, 86
Virtual Reality Modeling Language (VRML), 1, 88–89
warnings, 9
World Wide Web, 1
Yahoo!, 35, 39